It Isn't The Way We Think It Is

Seven Common Beliefs That Aren't in the Bible

LES BURCH

TATE PUBLISHING
AND ENTERPRISES, LLC

Published by Tate Publishing & Enterprises, LLC
127 E. Trade Center Terrace | Mustang, Oklahoma 73064 USA
1.888.361.9473 | www.tatepublishing.com

Tate Publishing is committed to excellence in the publishing industry. The company reflects the philosophy established by the founders, based on Psalm 68:11,
"The Lord gave the word and great was the company of those who published it."

Book design copyright © 2013 by Tate Publishing, LLC. All rights reserved.
Cover design by Joel Uber
Interior design by Jomel Pepito

Published in the United States of America
ISBN: 978-1-62510-749-7
1. Religion / Christian Theology / General
2. Religion / Christian Life / General
13.05.06

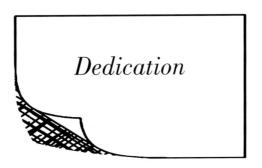

Dedication

To my wife, Carol, who wrapped our boys in care and still covers them in prayer; to our boys, Jeff and Nick, who seek to live God's truth beyond any measure I could have taught; to my mother, Alice, who put me on the path of unquestioned faith in God and His word.

Acknowledgment

I am anxious to give credit to a pioneer who helped me re-look at things and step out of the normal theological box. I owe much to the writings of A. E. Knoch and his accurate translation, the *Concordant Literal Version*. Here was a man dedicated to the Word of God and fearless in following truth. Much of what he learned was a result of the meticulous and laborious work of translation. Mr. Knoch was not paid to do this. He belonged to no denomination and financed most of the work himself. His goal was to produce a work as faithful to the original languages as possible. Though he had changes in his own theology as a result, he did not want bias in the translation. He wanted only to present the most accurate translation so that the reader had the closest possible connection with God's Word. I believe he accomplished that, and I recommend the *Concordant Literal Version* highly.[1] It puts you as near to the original language as possible without having to learn the original Greek or Hebrew.

---

[1]   Concordant Publishing, Almont, MI *(http://www.concordant. org)*

Table of Contents

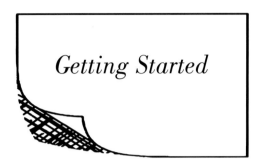

Getting Started

Years ago, I came across a verse I really didn't like. It created a conflict inside. The only thing I did right was to accept that it was God's truth, but it took several more years to understand it and embrace it as right. What if you realized that some of the Christian tenets you and your friends hold dear don't agree with the Bible? Would that shake you or could you see it as an adventure?

I used to believe that God ran the universe sort of like a watch. He wound it up and then pretty much left it alone, returning only to see how it was running. But the more I read the Scripture, the more I realized that God works constantly in real time. Finding that He is the Real-Time God was a big change for me. Can you change long-held notions and still be okay?

Is your foundation built on inherited beliefs or what God has said? Would it seem too fantastic that we have been influenced as much by generations of cultural traditions as we have by God's Word? The early church at Berea was praised because they "searched the Scriptures daily to find out whether these things were so."[2]

---

[2]   Acts 17:11

You may ask, "What difference does it make if I believe something that isn't exactly true as long as I am saved?" Paul spent much of his adult life exhorting the early church to stay with the truth and avoid false teaching.[3] He was concerned enough to face Peter with the hypocrisy of teaching Gentiles to observe Jewish traditions, which would take away their freedom in Christ.[4] Paul did not accuse Peter and others of not being saved but of not upholding the truth of the gospel.

Wasn't it Jesus who said, "The truth shall set you free"?[5] To whatever extent we believe a lie, we are in bondage to it. It is well worth the struggle for each of us to filter out man-made notions and embrace God's words.

We can get off track by trusting our intuition and reasoning. Even good logic can fail us when we don't start with the right information. Earlier generations believed in a sun that revolved around the earth—quite a reasonable conclusion from normal observation. It comes up over here and goes down over there. Over and over and over the sun repeats its path around the earth. And by the way, the earth is flat because it sure looks flat from where I'm standing. And since the stars seem to rotate through a predictable cycle relative to the earth, the earth must be not only the center for the sun and moon but also the center of the universe.

Put yourself in that time when the majority of people bought into the idea of a flat earth that was in the center of the universe. I can hear the crowd now, "How can you think the earth is round when everyone around you disagrees? What makes you think you are right? Do you alone have a corner on the truth?" We now extol the virtues of those who went against the prevailing

---

[3]   Galatians 2:4-5
[4]   Galatians 2:14
[5]   John 8:32

thought. Even with best intentions, the majority opinion—even a Christian majority—can be wrong.

Our human viewpoint (like the world looks flat) isn't always reliable. Sometimes the truth is backwards. It's counter intuitive. If you want to save your life, lose it. If you want joy, join in suffering. If you want to end up in the east, travel west. God's ways are not our ways.[6]

Are you ready to consider some opinions that run counter to traditional Christian thought? I hope so, and I hope that you would only be willing if there were good evidence. Although it can sometimes be fun, difference for difference's sake is no virtue.

The problem with the old earth-centric theories, of course, was that under closer observation all the pieces didn't fit. People began to realize after many centuries, "It isn't the way we think it is."

And perhaps even more to the point, at times, it isn't the way we want it to be. There is not only a logic to current beliefs, but there is also an emotional attachment, a comfort zone of sorts. The truth can be far more surprising and, in some ways, upsetting. Earth was not to be the center of the universe and by implication, perhaps, neither were we. We don't like the new answer. It gives us a smaller position of importance, and we are attached to importance.

This book is about the workings of God and of life and questions we sometimes have. Are there things that have bothered you about your Christian beliefs and doctrines? Maybe you have been afraid to voice seeming inconsistencies in the belief systems you were taught. Perhaps you have voiced them but felt silenced, didn't get an answer that satisfied, or maybe were even told your questioning was wrong. If any of that resonates with you, this just might be a good book for you.

---

[6]   Isaiah 55:8-9

The subjects in each chapter aren't necessarily related and neither do they have any chronology. That means if you are a browser, you can start reading anyplace.

Within these chapters are some of the great questions of life, and maybe that is why they interest me and I hope will interest you. You need to know that I write from a Christian perspective, believing in God's Word as ultimate truth. I do not seek to defend that position; I simply take it as a given. I can promise you that you will read biblical perspectives that you have rarely, if ever, come across. People can get quite excited and, at times, very agitated when you mess with their theology. New answers, even if they fit better, disrupt a world made secure through familiarity. If you find yourself in that corner, it could be a bumpy ride. My advice is to have fun with it, and give it a good go. God is well able to defend Himself, and we will find out soon enough how little we have really pieced together. Some chapters do not address such weighty matters and are just fun or interesting things to think about.

Though this book is a compendium of subjects, to say there isn't a theme or a common thread would be to deny the reason for it in the first place. It is essentially about the reverence of God's Word. It is about regarding God's words above the words of men. There are instances where men's ideas and words have crept into our beliefs as if they came from God.

Whether in the end, you agree with my interpretation or I agree with yours is not so important. I could not have written an entire book and gotten it all right as God measures right. I wish I could, and I wish I knew where it goes wrong. What is important is that we agree that God is right, whatever He meant. God's Word is holy. It is to be set apart in our minds and in our hearts.

Don't Mess with Texas was a familiar bumper sticker in the late '80s. It was a slogan meant to reduce littering on the highways, but the other meaning of a fun-loving Texas pride came through loud and clear.

Culturally speaking, you don't want to mess with Texas; spiritually speaking, you don't want to mess with God's Word.

> Every word of God [is] pure;
> He [is] a shield to those who put their trust in Him.
> Do not add to His words,
> Lest He rebuke you, and you be found a liar.
>
> Proverbs 30:5–6 (NKJV)

I love the purity and refinement of God's word.

> The words of the Lord [are] pure words,
> [Like] silver tried in a furnace of earth,
> Purified seven times.
>
> Psalm 12:6 (NKJV)

I also love to learn what God thinks about things.

> How precious also are Your thoughts to me, O God!
> How great is the sum of them!
>
> Psalm 139:17 (NKJV)

As a result, there is much Scripture contained in this book. Scripture quotations are to be read as part of the flow of thought. You may miss the point if you skip them. Italics within quoted verses are mine to emphasize the point being made. Wherever Scripture is referred to but not quoted in the text, it is footnoted at the bottom of the page instead of being referenced at the end of the chapter or book. This is to make it easy for you to stop if you wish and look it up.

I hope that *It Isn't the Way We Think It Is* will be a fun, challenging, and life-changing adventure. Let's get started!

Is Life Fair?

She was one of those second-class children deemed worthy only of rags and ashes while her sisters lived in spoiled ease on the back of her hard service. And for shouldering most of the work, her family treated her with contempt. Yet, no one in the community seemed to care enough to step in and rescue this beautiful and innocent girl. To see that kind of family injustice year after year is a grinding thing. It gnaws at our insides. It isn't fair. We yearn to right the wrong, to save the downtrodden, and, yes, to punish the offenders. The story of Cinderella has endured because it speaks of the unspeakable wrongs of favoritism.

> **Common Belief**
> *Life should be fair.*

Do you think life is fair? Do you expect it to be fair? In searching for answers, I find the majority of people conclude that life is unfair. Some struggle with getting the short end, others say "buck up and get through it," and still others conclude that life is actually fair because it is equally unfair to all. Rather than getting mired in the philosophical bog, let's just observe that people struggle with struggles and, to one degree or another, everyone seems to expect a fair shake.

To have an equal share, to be free from favoritism, to get what is deserved, to play according to the rules—these are the building blocks of fairness and the stepping stones that show us more clearly whether life is fair. Everyday get-up-in-the-morning, backpack-it-to-class, punch-in-at-work, and shop-at-the-mall life has all the evidence we need.

Look around you. If you deem that fairness is all about equality, you will have a difficult search indeed. Who has started life with the same talents? No one you know. The same circumstances? Not a chance. What about the same health or wealth? Physical appearance? Mental abilities? Is there anything you can think of that is fair and equal between humans? Before we even begin to do good or bad, before we even deserve prize or prison, we start the race of life all over the track with no hint of an even starting line. Later in life, we learn to ask for a fair playing field, realizing that it didn't start that way.

It is easy for children to feel that favoritism is at work in their family. We have all had those feelings from time to time. To some it seems that siblings aren't punished as harshly for the same offenses or they get more of the good stuff. Like Cinderella, once in a while it is true. It can be so starkly true that everyone around can see it, and hearts go out to those unjustly degraded. Nothing seems so wrong as a father's wrath on one child while his blessing is consistently on another. Stepmothers and stepfathers alike have long had the reputation (often deserved) of slighting the children not their own.

Some people we would deem the salt of the earth experience the greatest tragedies. They deserve better. It doesn't seem fair. I know a great Christian lady who is always of positive spirits and humble attitude. About six months after she lost her mother, her husband died of cancer. She rose out of it and maintained her positive faith in God. A few years later, her son hung himself from a bridge. There are no words. Why do bad things happen to good people? It does not seem fair.

Our passion for sports carries a strongly shared value of playing by the rules. We take a dim view of athletic achievements undergirded by steroids or of throwing the World Series on a wager. Beyond sports, we find that all walks of life have understood rules and all of them are routinely broken: the widescreen is returned to the store the day after Super Bowl, the transmission shop makes unneeded repairs, the expensive carpet is purchased but the cheaper look-alike delivered, test answers as phone text fly across the classroom, several movies are seen without buying new tickets. There are thousands of ways to cheat the system, millions of ways to break the rules, and always someone gets the unfair end of the deal.

If we start life from birth unfairly, it bothers us. It shouldn't be that way. We expect fairness. We expect it even more from the happenstance and circumstance of life. We have accepted the frailty of mankind—that we cheat and are cheated, that we lie and are lied to. But it is difficult to accept the luck of the draw. We fight against it. A girl is driven to *why-me* depression because her promiscuous sister with an attitude lands a great job, finds a great guy, and lives in the high-rise condo, while she yet lives with her parents, friendless, and dollarless.

We may agree that life is unfair, but we reserve the right to kickabout it. When we hear ourselves thinking, "It's unfair," "Why her?," "Why me?," or "Why did God allow?," we betray our real expectation that things ought to be fair. At times I do it, you do it, we all do it; we get into complaining that something isn't fair, it isn't the way things ought to be. Whether we argue about a minor inconvenience of life or struggle with a deep tragedy, we reveal our underlying expectation that things ought to be fair. The tighter and longer we cling to that expectation the more skeptical, bitter, and generally miserable we become. We need to recognize the errors we are making.

> *Life doesn't run on our timing*

If you believe in God, you know that life doesn't run on our timing or by our wishes; it runs on God's timing and by His choices. The fact that our railing against circumstances is actually railing against God is buried in the subconscious. Yet, sometimes, we lash out at God directly. Either way, we make four fundamental errors in our belief system, some we would rather not admit. Down deep we think that:

1. God should play by our rules.
2. God should play by the rules He gives us.
3. God should play by His own rules.
4. God is unjust.

We'll take a closer look into each.

God Should Play by Our Rules

Equal pay for equal work was a demand in the United States beginning in the early twentieth century. It was a cry for government legislation to require, monitor, and ensure that the employer paid each employee exactly the same pay for the same work. Appropriately, the legislation was known as The Fair Labor Standards Act of 1938. To this day, the fight for fairness in pay has not stopped. And who would disagree? Fair is fair.

If we, sinful as we are, have agreed on the very democratic and classless notion that pay structures should be equal, then God certainly would do no less. After all, it is one of our finest rules.

Matthew, the guy who collected taxes, relates a story told by Jesus about this very subject. It seems a vineyard keeper needed to hire some folks to pick grapes. A few started first thing in the morning of a long twelve-hour workday and agreed to labor that day for one silver coin—a denarius. Others came along during the day and were also put to work, trusting their pay would be fair, until in the most extreme case, one laborer was hired on with only one hour left in the work day. At the end of the day when they lined up to receive wages, how were the laborers paid? Did they each get the proportional amount of a denarius according to where the sun hit the dial?

> So when evening had come, the owner of the vineyard said to his steward, "Call the laborers and give them [their] wages, beginning with the last to the first." And when those came who [were] [hired] about the eleventh hour, they each received a denarius. But when the first came, they supposed that they would receive more; and they likewise received each a denarius. And when they had received [it], they complained against the landowner, saying, "These last [men] have worked [only] one hour, and you made them equal to us who have borne the burden and the heat of the day." But he answered one of them and said, "Friend, I am doing you no wrong. Did you not agree with me for a denarius? Take [what] [is] yours and go your way. I wish to give to this last man [the] [same] as to you. Is it not lawful for me to do what I wish with my own things? Or is your eye evil because I am good?"
>
> Matthew 20:8–15 (NKJV)

There you have it, equal pay for unequal work. The Unfair Labor Standards Act of AD 31. God doesn't obey our rules. He seems to value the authority and choice of the master above our equality doctrine.

God Should Play by the Rules He Gives Us

We have read that "you shall not murder,"[7] is one of God's Ten Commandments chiseled in stone. Today, the Bible is widely distributed and His commandments known beyond Israel, else the other nations would still not understand God's requirements. Yet now we do understand them, and for the most part we understand their wisdom. So now we have God's wisdom, and

---

[7]   Exodus 20:13

we know what is right and what is wrong. And it is not right to murder. Since it isn't right to murder, we conclude that it isn't right for God to murder.

Since the days of Abraham's exit from the city of Ur, the hope of occupying the land of promise lived in the hearts of all Israel. But it wasn't until 500 years later that Moses freed them from Egypt and took them to the brink of the land. After forty years of living in tents and wandering aimlessly in a parched wasteland, any upgrade would have been welcome. The promised land was a lush and plentiful land filled with milk and honey, a thing of joy.

There was only one problem. Someone was already living there and had for centuries. Israel could not just move in. They had to take the land by the bloodshed of military force. What God told Israel to do doesn't sound so joyful to today's reader.

> We took all his cities at that time, and we utterly destroyed the men, women, and little ones of every city; we left none remaining.
>
> Deuteronomy 2:34 (NKJV)

And they couldn't do it too quickly or they wouldn't have the people needed to husband all that land. So the people of the land had to live, perhaps many years, in fear, waiting for the ax of Israel and its God to fall.[8]

Israel itself shrank back from completely fulfilling God's war commands. They did not utterly destroy the inhabitants of the land. It wasn't a pleasant task. This process of killing everyone from pregnant woman to nursing child wasn't a thing of joy.[9] We might understand God destroying the idol worshippers, the wicked of the day. Perhaps you are tuned into grace and would protest that, "It wasn't their sin as much as it was their unbelief."

---

[8]   Exodus 23:27-30
[9]   I Samuel 15:3

But aren't we even a bit bothered by killing the infants? Was that right? Was it fair? They hardly had a chance to do good or evil.

Even the adults were at a severe disadvantage. Israel was the chosen nation and that only because God chose them—and not because they were righteous.

> Therefore understand that the Lord your God is not giving you this good land to possess because of your righteousness, for you [are] a stiff-necked people.
>
> Deuteronomy 9:6 (NKJV)

The other nations were "without God in the world."[10] They had done their best to subdue the earth, to be fruitful, and to multiply.[11] For the rest of their conduct, well, they just didn't know any better. They made up their own gods, for God did not visit them. They had to make up their own rules for God did not tell them how to live.[12] They had no commandments as to right and wrong. Even Israel, having the whole law and God's presence, was habitually disobedient. We wonder where mercy and grace come into play. As much as we might want to, we cannot find the answer by finding fault with the people of these nations who were without God. Oh, they had plenty of faults, but so did Israel who was in possession of much more knowledge than the other nations. Many times, God thought heavily of wiping Israel out as well. So how can we find fault with the infants or even the unborn of the day? If you believe that these nations deserved destruction, that we can ultimately blame them, let's look at the reasons given by God.

---

[10]   Ephesians 2:12
[11]   Genesis 1:28
[12]   Deuteronomy 4:7-8

> For it was of the Lord to harden their hearts, that they should
> come against Israel in battle, that He might utterly destroy
> them, [and] that they might receive no mercy, but that He
> might destroy them, as the Lord had commanded Moses.
>
> Joshua 11:20 (NKJV)

The fact is God didn't want them to repent or make peace with Israel. What do we do when God doesn't seem nice? What God asked Israel to do to occupy the land, today we call genocide. It is murder on a mass scale.

Let's bring it home. If we were to follow God's mandate for Israel today (which we clearly have not been given), we would arm Israel to the teeth so they could blow up the Gaza strip, kill every Muslim man, woman and child in Jerusalem, tear down the dome of the rock, and rebuild God's temple. We shudder to think of it, but that was His mandate for Israel. Why? He promised them the land and it was His land to give. God is into ownership, we are into diplomacy.

If we go down the road of who deserves what, we can't justify His actions. If we try to measure God Himself by the laws He gives to us, we won't find an explanation. *Who are we to judge God?* It isn't a question of what men deserve. It is instead a question of God's purpose. God is not subject to the Ten Commandments; they are not rules for Him. The Creator has the right over His creation to give life and to take it back. And He is not wrong.

> The LORD brings death and makes alive;
> he brings down to the grave and raises up.
>
> 1 Samuel 2:6 (NIV)

Who are we to judge His actions?

God Should Play by His Own Rules

God gave Israel a host of laws on how to live and how to judge and administer justice. He made laws for giving and laws for washing, laws for eating and laws for resting. His resting law was to observe the weekly day of rest, the Sabbath, on which there was to be no occupational work in Israel. When creating the heavens and the earth, God Himself observed this law and rested on the seventh (Sabbath) day. In other words, it was a rule He set out for Himself before man was on the scene.

Then Jesus came along. He healed on the Sabbath. His disciples picked grain on the Sabbath.[13] There is no doubt that Jesus broke the Sabbath laws that God Himself followed. In the eyes of the Pharisees, Jesus was a lawbreaker.

Let's listen in on the argument:

> At that season Jesus went through the sowings on the Sabbaths. Now His disciples hunger, and they begin to be plucking the ears and to be eating. Now the Pharisees, perceiving it, say to Him, "Lo! Your disciples are doing what is not allowed to be done on a Sabbath." Yet He said to them, "Did you not read what David does when he hungers, and those with him: how he entered into the house of God and they ate the show bread, which he was not allowed to eat, neither those with him, except the priests only? Or did you not read in the law that on the Sabbaths the priests in the sanctuary are profaning the Sabbath and are faultless? Now I am saying to you that a Greater than the sanctuary is here. Now if you had known what this is: Mercy am I wanting, and not sacrifice—you would not convict the faultless, for the Son of Mankind is Lord of the Sabbath."
>
> Matthew 12:1–8 (CLV)

---

[13]   Matthew 12:1-10

The Pharisees expected God and anyone representing God to obey the Sabbath law as God Himself had done. They saw Jesus as the lawbreaker not the lawmaker; they could not see that "Greater than the sanctuary is here." The very one who spoke them into existence is here. When the rule maker is in town, the rules are up for grabs. Is this right? Is it fair not to play by the rules? Perhaps a down-to-earth example would help.

Computers are wonderful creations. They almost have a mind of their own. In fact, today's operating systems are amazing. The foremost was created by Bill Gates and was designed to give standard instructions to the computer. Many different companies make the hardware portion of the computer, but they all obey the same instructions, the rules of computer life. Without them our computers would be chaos. Each computer must have the instructions loaded into its circuitry before it is of any use.

Many of the rules given to computers are about what they can't do. As an example, they are not to write over information on a disc unless they are specifically told they can. If the disc is protected, they can't do it at all. And Gates said, "You shall not overwrite." And it was so. When the computers learned and used this instruction they were happy. Can you imagine how upset the computers might be if Bill Gates came in and overwrote a protected disc? They would be indignant. "Error! Error! Illegal Operation! Shut down all programs and reboot!"

There is something about the instructions the computers didn't learn. Bill Gates does not have to obey them. He created the rules, and he can break them. They are not rules for Bill Gates; they are the rules for computers. It is quite all right if Bill Gates decides to overwrite a disk. He knows what he is doing.

Why don't we give our Creator the same courtesy? Why don't we understand that the rule maker is not constrained even by rules He has once followed and that is okay?

God Is Unjust

My hero has always been Job, Old Testament Job. He doesn't have the awe-inspiring miracles of Moses or the swashbuckling adventures of David; but when it comes to reacting in faith, obedience, and worship in the face of heartbreaking disaster, Job is second to none.

Job lost it all in one solitary day: his children, his servants, his cattle. Of all he loved and possessed, only his wife was left, but as it turned out she was there more to heckle than to comfort. And what did Job say to all of this?

> Then Job arose, tore his robe, and shaved his head; and he fell to the ground and worshiped. And he said: "Naked I came from my mother's womb, And naked shall I return there. The Lord gave, and the Lord has taken away; Blessed be the name of the Lord."
>
> Job 1:20–21 (NKJV)

I ask myself, could I react like that to even a much milder tragedy? Would I not question God? Would I not blame God?

There is much that is interesting and revealing about this whole story. It is one of the few incidents of Scripture that allows us to peer behind the scenes. We get to go backstage to see the forces and personalities behind the events.

Right off the bat, we are told what kind of guy this Job was.

> There was a man in the country of Uz. Job was his name. And this man was flawless and upright, fearing Elohim and withdrawing from evil.
>
> Job 1:1 (CLV)

This is not man's opinion of Job; it is God's opinion. Then God, for reasons we cannot hear even from our position behind the curtain, begins to stir the pot.

Then the Lord said to Satan, "Have you considered My servant Job, that there] [is] none like him on the earth, a blameless and upright man, one who fears God and shuns evil?" So Satan answered the Lord and said, "Does Job fear God for nothing?"

Job 1:8–9 (NKJV)

Now if you were Job behind the curtain, you might not like this too much. It's like when they are looking for volunteers and you try to be really small but everybody points to you anyway. Things were going along well. God said so Himself. Job was an upright man who shunned evil. God had blessed him with many sons and daughters and lots of cattle. If you were Job, you were not really looking for many changes. Why does God egg Satan on? Satan had plenty else to occupy his time. And so as it would seem, a little wager begins.

"Have you yourself not hedged him about, and about his house and about all that is his all around. The work of his hands you have blessed, and his cattle breach forth throughout the countryside. Howbeit, now put forth your hand and touch all that is his. He shall assuredly scorn you to your face." Hence Yahweh said to Satan, "Behold, all that he has is in your hand, but you must not put forth your hand upon himself." Then Satan went forth from Yahweh's presence.

Job 1:10–12 (CLV)

So God points Satan in Job's direction and, to boot, takes down the protective wall. "Have at him!" So "Satan went forth" all right, and he destroyed Job's family and his possessions in one day.[14] Job's reaction was immediate. He didn't have to think, "Now I should be holy and react in faith."

---

[14]   Job 1:13-19

And he said: "Naked I came from my mother's womb, And naked shall I return there. The Lord gave, and the Lord has taken away; Blessed be the name of the Lord."

Job 1:21 (NKJV)

This is, to me, an unbelievable and unreachable state of subjection to God. Were I to attain one tenth of this faith I would consider myself blessed beyond reason. We know that Job did not curse God and that Satan was then allowed to harm him physically, short of death. But still Job did not curse God. Then entered Job's wife. To be fair, she underwent the same pain of loss other than his physical ailments. Unlike Job, however, she blamed and did not bless.

Then his wife said to him, "Do you still hold fast to your integrity? Curse God and die!" But he said to her, "You speak as one of the foolish women speaks. Shall we indeed accept good from God, and shall we not accept adversity?" In all this, Job did not sin with his lips.

Job 2:9–10 (NKJV)

Now there are two very crucial things we must pull from this verse. They go a long way in answering this whole subject of God and the unfairness of evil events. Some, in defending God, point to Satan as the perpetrator in order to absolve God from blame. This is not easily defensible from the text though many a theology needs it. It is plain enough that God was at the controls. Remember that Satan retorted back to God, "Stretch out Your hand and touch all that he has."[15] Stretch out whose hand? God's! Though Satan was the tool, even he recognized that it was ultimately God's hand that would strike Job. And notice something else. Satan had limits. He could not at this time touch Job himself. And Satan obeyed God's limits. Satan is not pictured

---

[15]   Job 1:11

here as some loose cannon, an adversary of God's going headlong after his own agenda. But we don't need our own interpretation; Job himself answers it for us.

"In all this, Job did not sin with his lips." In all what? In saying, "Shall we indeed accept good from God and shall we not accept adversity?" In other words, Job does not lay this on Satan but instead he credits God for the evil. And in laying this disaster upon God, Job does not sin with his lips. God accepts this responsibility as right. This very statement of Job's is preserved so that we know it is okay to trace adversity back to God. No doubt Satan was the messenger, the tool, the pawn, but Job knows from whom it came. "Have you considered my servant Job?"

The second thing to know I recently learned it myself in presenting this topic to a group. You may still be uncomfortable in blaming God for evil. I used to use this word *blame*, thinking that after all, God was ultimately responsible. And He is responsible. That He caused this evil to Job is quite plain. But as I learned, blame is another matter. We can't blame God because this word carries with it the charge of wrong or guilt. To blame someone is to also hold them at fault or charge them with sin. God did not sin in bringing disaster on Job. Job did not sin either. He did not blame God. In his reaction to the loss of his children and cattle, we know he was humble, yet he gave God the credit as the Source.

> The Lord gave, and the Lord has taken away; Blessed be the name of the Lord." In all this Job did not sin nor charge God with wrong.
>
> Job 1:21–22 (NKJV)

I used to concentrate on verse 21, yet verse 22 completes the truth. Job was not charging God with wrong. He simply said that God was responsible that verse 20 asserts was the worshipful thing to do. He was recognizing God's right as Creator to give and to take, to do as He wishes with His creation. Still, it seems so arbitrary and senseless. Surely, this is an isolated case, and we shouldn't use it to generalize as if God routinely brings arbitrary evil into our lives, right? Perhaps this case isn't so isolated.

Enter Esau and Jacob, twins of Isaac and Rebecca, Esau being the elder. Now, in God's law the elder would inherit a double portion and, eventually, be the patriarch of the family; that was the birthright of the firstborn.

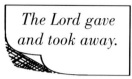

The Lord gave and took away.

> For though [the twins] were not yet born, and had not done anything good or bad, in order that God's purpose according to [His] choice might stand, not because of works, but because of Him who calls, it was said to her, "The older will serve the younger." Just as it is written, "Jacob I loved, but Esau I hated."
>
> Romans 9:11–13 (NASB)

"Jacob I loved, but Esau I hated." Esau is Cinderella. God doesn't like him very much, and it is hard for us to take. In fact, many try to justify God's choice by claiming that Esau deserved God's wrath. There are two good reasons why this doesn't wash.

Verse 11 (above) makes it painfully plain. God made His choice to love one and hate the other before they were ever born. It makes a specific point of saying that neither had done anything good or bad when God made His choice. It emphasizes good and bad so that we know that Esau hadn't done anything bad to deserve God's hatred and Jacob had done nothing good to deserve His love. Still there are those who can't stand it and claim that God knew that Esau would be bad, and therefore, God is justified in His choice.

Whatever we think of Esau, Jacob certainly wasn't a fellow of sterling character. He was a conniver and a swindler. He pressured Esau out of his birthright and cheated him out of his blessing. There was nothing in Jacob to deserve God's love. We can't justify God's choice by the actions of the two brothers. On top of that, by choosing Jacob, God countermanded His own law of the firstborn.

It would be unjust for us to show such favoritism, and when God does it we are tempted to declare that, "God is unjust!" He knows how we think.

> What then shall we say? Is God unjust? Not at all!
>
> Romans 9:14 (NIV)

Despite the appearances of injustice, we aren't to think that way; we aren't to say that God is unjust. But isn't it contradictory to God's own instruction to us to judge without favoritism?

> To show partiality to the wicked is not good, Or to turn aside the righteous in judgment.
>
> Proverbs 18:5 (CLV)

Who Are You?

Don't show favoritism to the rich, or don't put down the poor in your judgments. These are the right guides for us. Cinderella should be treated as any other family member. It is only fair. Are these the same guidelines for God? Are we to hold Him to a *fairness* standard?

> On the contrary, who are you, O man, who answers back to God? The thing molded will not say to the molder, "Why did you make me like this," will it?
>
> Romans 9:20 (NASB)

Protest as we might, that is the answer. I must confess that for many years I didn't like this answer. I believed it, but I didn't like it. When God does something that violates our sense of justice— even the justice that He taught us—His answer is, "Who are you?" At first, that might not satisfy you either. But it needs to.

It is God's answer. What might be unjust for us is not unjust for God.

> Or has not the potter the right over the clay, out of the same kneading to make one vessel, indeed, for honor, yet one for dishonor?
>
> Romans 9:21 (CLV)

One pot for honor and the other for dishonor; it is His choice, and it doesn't depend on the pot. When you think about it, we do the same thing. Out of the same porcelain, we will craft a fine teapot and a toilet; one vessel for honor, the other for dishonor. It isn't the porcelain's choice, it is ours, and it has nothing to do with the porcelain being naughty or nice.

Jacob for honor, Esau for dishonor—that the choice of God might stand.[16] We wouldn't have done it that way. We would have given it to the deserving one, the loyal and faithful and upright one. But maybe, just maybe, it isn't the way we think it is.

God asked Israel to wipe out thousands in order that they might inhabit the land of promise. And He was not wrong. Still, sorrow must have mixed with joy when Jericho fell. To do what God bids and to see it as right is a matter of faith. It is not always an easy road. We want to hold Him to the standards that He has given us as if we were the lawgivers.

My son Jeffrey took a psychology course in high school taught by a college professor. In the class, he wrote a paper on moral philosophy that got into quite a discussion of right and wrong and moral absolutes tied to God as the source. When he got the paper back, the professor had jotted a question in the margin. "Did God do it because it was right, or was it right because God did it?"

It was a good question. I am guessing, but I think the professor asked it because he thought it was one of those unanswerable

---

[16]   Romans 9:11

questions. But for anyone who believes in God, it must be answered. It is a crucial question.

There can be no correct answer other than it was right because God did it. God defines what is right. There is no right outside of God. What He does is right simply because He does it. The universe does not define God; God defines the universe. The laws of science are not natural laws. They are God's laws. There cannot be a system or a structure that is above God. It is a contradiction in terms. The title itself, *God* means the one to whom all is subjected. If the laws and rules He established constrain Him, then He is subject to them and is not God.

What He does with His creation is right. It is not wrong. God had His reasons for what He did with Job and His choice between Jacob and Esau. God doesn't need us to defend His character. He doesn't want our absolution, to somehow fit words to justify Him. He wants our total submission and obedience. He wants our faith in Him that what He does is righteous and right.

God is right

Is Death Fair?

As Bill Cosby has said of his right as a father, "I brought you into this world and I can take you out!" Well said. God has brought us into this world, and He can take us out. In fact, He will take us out.

Yes, one way or the other, we are all leaving. One way or the other, we will all die. To see someone die young is a double tragedy. We are most sorrowful over a teen dying or a young child of four or five. It seems very unfair for them to pass away in the flower of youth or for life to slip away from a newborn just hours out of the womb. When a person of eighty or ninety goes "the way of all the earth,"[17] we are saddened but we don't tend to think

---

[17]   Joshua 23:14

it unfair. We expect it. We have seen it often. Someday, the enemy of death will come.

We are so conditioned to it that we tell ourselves that it is okay for one so full of years. But why is death, in the end, so different for the young than for the old? Isn't it all tragic? Isn't death an enemy at any age? Where is the line? Is death less tragic at eighty than at seventy? How about sixty-five or fifty-five? Would we feel okay with God when someone of fifty dies, or can it be all right at forty-two? Do you see the problem? We have a sliding scale based on when people die or how people die. The real unfairness (and I am posing this from the human viewpoint because God is not unfair) is that anybody dies at all.

The real issue, the core issue, the critical issue is not when people die or how people die. It is that people do die. It doesn't make much sense to label the death of a child unfair or the death of innocent victims unjust when everyone, sooner or later, is condemned to death. Which is more fair? To die of disease or to die in a collapsing building? While we wrestle with issues of God's fairness around certain tragic events, we totally miss the larger issue. Is death itself unfair? When is death fair? Is the whole issue of sin and death even a matter of fairness? Fairness may not turn out to be the issue that we think it is.

Of all the unfair deaths of the world, one stands alone as the worst in history. Christ, the very Son of God, was crucified. There has been no other evil so blatantly wrong by fairness standards. He was sinless amongst a world of sinners. He was blameless against a world of guilty accusers. In his mouth was no guile and lying mouths surrounded him.[18]

Yet, God not only gave Him up to be dishonored, spat upon, and crucified, but He planned it in advance.

> But with the precious blood of Christ, as of a lamb without blemish and without spot. He indeed was foreordained

---

[18]   1 Peter 2:22-23

before the foundation of the world, but was manifest in these last times for you

1 Peter 1:19–20 (NKJV)

Those who followed Christ did not understand His coming death. It felt very wrong. How could these arrogant ruffians kill their King and Lord? Peter went to lengths to protect our Lord from it and was rebuked for his actions as a messenger of Satan.

Then Peter took Him aside and began to rebuke Him, saying, "Far be it from You, Lord; this shall not happen to You!" But He turned and said to Peter, "Get behind Me, Satan! You are an offense to Me, for you are not mindful of the things of God, but the things of men."

Matthew 16:22–23 (NKJV)

What is Peter's error? Not being mindful of the things of God. Life on this planet is just not a matter of fairness as we would have it. If it were, we would all live the same number of days and die in our sleep. Instead, our days are numbered by someone else.

Your eyes saw my embryo, And my days, all of them were written upon Your scroll; The days were formed when there was not one of them.

Psalm 139:16 (CLV)

It is true we carry greater sadness when the young perish, but if we wrestle with God over fairness it should be the larger issue of death itself. Why do people die? If they didn't, all the other questions of dying young or dying painfully would disappear.

Why do we die? You know the answer.

Therefore, even as through one man sin entered into the world, and through sin death, and thus death passed through into all mankind.

Romans 5:12 (CLV)

From Adam we inherited death and it includes all humanity. If fairness is all about equality, then death is fair; we are all in the club. If it is about what we deserve, it is very unfair since death is an inherited gene, and there is absolutely nothing we can do about it. Though none of us knows exactly when, we all have the appointment.

> And as it is appointed for men to die once.
>
> Hebrews 9:27 (NKJV)

God knows the day of our birth and the day of our death when "there was not one of them."[19] That means He must know the very day a youth will die and the very day innocent victims will perish. And we should not cry to God, "Unfair!" Death of any sort is tragic, and we have a right to mourn and to grieve but not to accuse God of unfairness or wrongdoing.

Our error is like Peter's error. Not being mindful of the things of God. What looks terribly wrong and unfair is in concert with the things of God. Is death fair? In the end, it is not a matter of fairness but of God's choice.

Death, however, does have a purpose that God has revealed to us. It is not arbitrary and capricious, and it is not a somber end.

> Yes, we had the sentence of death in ourselves, that we should not trust in ourselves but in God who raises the dead.
>
> 2 Corinthians 1:9 (NKJV)

The finality of death causes us to trust totally in God. We cannot loose the pangs of death;[20] we cannot raise ourselves to

---

[19]   Psalm 139:16
[20]   Acts 2:24

newness of life;[21] we cannot, like a new coat, put on immortality.[22] But He can.

Is Life Fair?

We often think of fairness in the context of the negative or hurtful events in our lives. What about the positives? Do we not take them for granted? Are the good things we have gotten fair and the bad things unfair?

We think it unfair if we are overcharged but don't give fairness a thought when we get something for free. When right answers are marked wrong, it is unfair; but when we get a higher grade than we deserve, we lucked out.

If fairness is about getting what we deserve, then it must apply to the good things too. Do we deserve a birthday party? Christmas presents? A warm fire? When we've worked hard, we believe we deserve a vacation. Do we? Is it fair? Do people get vacations in proportion to the hours or difficulty of work they put in? The truth is, the good things just seem to come to us with no rhyme or reason. But is it fair that we get them?

Is it fair that we have life itself? Did we deserve life? Did you deserve life? If you did, then what exactly did you do to deserve birth? Statistically, anyone who made it into this world won the lottery. Each time a human egg is successfully fertilized there were about 200 million sperm in the contest and you won! It was an almost impossible victory of greater than Olympic proportions. With those kinds of odds, a person has to feel lucky to be here. But what about the little guy behind you? Was it fair that it was you and not him?

Do we get what we deserve?

---

21   Romans 6:4
22   I Corinthians 15:53

There is no answer to that, other than it was in the Creator's heart to put you here. Your purpose for being here cannot be your own; it must be tied up in His purpose for you. The fact that you were given life, good things to eat, clothes on your back, and shelter over your head isn't fair or deserved. It just is. Don't you sometimes wonder why God has given you things that you think others deserve more?

He is the potter and we are the clay. Is there a better analogy to show our place in the universe? We are tools in the Creator's hand. Is life fair? It is the wrong question. The better question is, "Who created me, and what does He want?"

> `Now see that I, [even] I, [am] He,
> And [there] [is] no God besides Me;
> I kill and I make alive;
> I wound and I heal;
> Nor [is] [there] [any] who can deliver from My hand.
>
> Deuteronomy 32:39 (NKJV)

Are we left in despair? If we are to give up fairness, if we are to give up seeking why the tragedies of life befall us, if there is no answer to the suffering of the innocent, then is there no mercy, no kindness, no reprieve.

Must we give up altogether our sense and desire that things be made right? I don't think so. God has not given us the understanding of right and wrong or the desire to see evil conquered for no reason. We, after all, did not think up the idea of righteousness and good on our own.

The story of Job finishes well. It finishes the way we want to see the movie end.

> Then Yahweh Himself turned back the captivity of Job when he prayed on behalf of his associates. And Yahweh added to all that Job had by a double portion. All his brothers and all his sisters came to him and all his acquaintances from before, and they ate bread with him in his house. Then

they sympathized with him and comforted him over all
the evil that Yahweh had brought upon him. Each of them
gave to him one kesitah, and each, one pendant of gold.
Thus Yahweh Himself blessed the latter years of Job more
than his beginning. He came to have a flock of fourteen
thousand sheep, six thousand camels, a thousand pair of
oxen and a thousand jennies. Also he came to have seven
sons and three daughters.

Job 42:10–13 (CLV)

We would have thought the evil God brought upon Job grossly
unfair. But Job's end was better than his beginning. Not only did
he get back a double portion, he got something much more. Job
received a lesson in who God is.

So Yahweh answered Job from the tempest and said: Belt
up your loins then like a master; I shall ask of you, and you
inform Me. Indeed, would you ever annul My judgment?
Would you condemn Me that you might be justified? Do
you have an arm like El's? And can you thunder with a
voice like His?

Job 40:6–9 (CLV)

It is hard to imagine that one as blameless and humble as Job
had something more to learn. I suspect we have a lot to learn
with him.

Then Job replied to the LORD: "I know that you can do
all things; no plan of yours can be thwarted. [You asked,]
'Who is this that obscures my counsel without knowledge?'
Surely I spoke of things I did not understand, things too
wonderful for me to know. ["You said,] 'Listen now, and I
will speak; I will question you, and you shall answer me.'
My ears had heard of you but now my eyes have seen you.
Therefore I despise myself and repent in dust and ashes."

Job 42:1–6 (NIV)

Would we condemn God? Would we question His treatment of Job, His hatred of Esau, His destruction of the people of the land? Esau did not get the blessing from his father Isaac or from God. He was not to be in the direct line of the chosen people. Yet in the end, we see God granting him blessing.

> And I give to Isaac, Jacob and Esau; and I give to Esau mount Seir, to possess it; and Jacob and his sons have gone down to Egypt.
>
> Joshua 24:4 (CLV)

God not only gave Esau the inheritance of Seir but he moved to protect that gift. He would not let even the chosen of Jacob come against it.

> And instruct the people saying, You shall pass through the territory of your brothers, the sons of Esau, who are dwelling in Seir. They shall fear you, yet you must be very much on guard. Do not stir yourselves up against them, for I shall not give to you any of their country, not even a tread of a foot's sole—for I have given the hill-country of Seir for a tenancy to Esau.
>
> Deuteronomy 2:4–5 (CLV)

Our problem is that we watch the middle of the movie and quit. We don't like what we see so we don't look beyond. We see Superman weakened by kryptonite, Batman trapped by a scheming Penguin, and 007 tricked by a wily double agent. We seem to stop at sin, punishment, and judgment. Why do we dwell at the low point and turn off the set in despair?

We watch the middle of the movie then quit

We concentrate on this life only. What about resurrection; what about immortality, what about wiping away every tear? The Apostle Paul would assert:

If we are having an expectation in Christ in this life only,
more forlorn than all men are we.

1 Corinthians 15:19 (CLV)

It isn't over. It's only the middle of the movie.

Christ's death brought life. Not only for Him but also for all those who believe in His name. An unspeakable wrong brought unfathomable good.

Who Himself carries up our sins in His body on to the pole, that, coming away from sins, we should be living for righteousness; by Whose welt you were healed.

1 Peter 2:24 (CLV)

God will bring final victory to pass. And unlike our superheroes, He will relieve us once for all time from fighting the battle without and the battle within. The greater news is the victory has already been won. It is complete and will come to pass.

Whom God raises, loosing the pangs of death, forasmuch as it was not possible for Him to be held by it.

Acts 2:24 (CLV)

God restores Job, gives Esau an inheritance, blesses all nations, and raises Christ from the dead, giving Him the name that is above every name. He abolishes the last enemy, death.[23] Yes, eventually the sense of right and wrong and fairness God taught us and the promise of grace and mercy we believe in is performed by God.

For there is only a moment under His anger.

But a lifetime under His benevolence.
In the evening, lamentation may lodge,
But in the morning there is jubilant song.

Psalm 30:5 (CLV)

---

[23]   I Corinthians 15:26

It may take a long while, and it may not come in this lifetime. Nevertheless it comes.

> Then shall come to pass the word which is written, Swallowed up was Death by Victory.
>
> 1 Corinthians 15:54b (CLV)

The next time the sadness of life closes in, when it narrows your vision and makes you believe how few your options are, how bleak the future and how desperate the moment, ask yourself, "How was it that life came upon me? How did it find me and place me on the globe? What great power and design must have formed my heart and planted my thoughts? What great purpose did this builder have, and how fortunate am I to be given life, to fill my lungs in the crisp night air, and to look up at the starry canvas, the little specks of light millions of miles distant finding a way to my sight, each magically suspended in dark void? To have the gift of awareness, the feel of raw ground beneath my feet, to see beauty I cannot explain, to hear the laughters and rhythms and songs of all that joins me in living?" Life is a gift we cannot measure, and the life to come one we cannot imagine.

> For I am reckoning that the sufferings of the current era do not deserve the glory about to be revealed for us.
>
> Romans 8:18 (CLV)

The glories about to be revealed are not fair; they are lavish and extravagant. To question the fairness of life is to question God Himself, and who are we to talk back to God? It is ours simply to trust and obey—for there is really no other way.

To know the Creator, to love the Creator, and to believe the Creator is the ultimate aim for His creatures. The Lord has given, the Lord has taken away, and the Lord will give a double portion. Blessed be the name of the Lord.

Reflections

1. Give one example where God broke a rule.
2. Do you believe what God did to Job was unjust? Why or why not?
3. What is God's answer to us when He does something we think is unfair? Is this answer difficult for you? Explain.
4. What is fair about death?
5. What is fair about life?

Could I Love an Ugly Jesus?

This is Jesus; kind, courageous, caring, and strong. Can you follow Him? Can you love Him?

I have often wondered how I would act, what I would do, and how I would feel if I encountered the walking, talking, in-front-of-your-face Jesus. Have you wondered that?

Not long ago, my wife and I stood in our church congregation, singing along as the band led. My eyes wandered, measuring the attractiveness and dress code of people on stage. One woman stood out to me. She was pear shaped and heavier than the other band members. The almost unconscious thought dashed through, "I wonder what she is doing up there?"

Fresh realization came over me that Sunday: how much I

> **Common Belief**
>
> *Jesus is a handsome guy with long hair.*

still used appearance to judge others. A bigger question began to sink in: How might I have judged the earthly Jesus?

Somehow, we all know what Jesus looks like. We can tell his picture easily with no caption needed. Modern depictions are amazingly consistent one to the other. He has wavy, long hair; the strength of a square jaw and high cheekbones. His skin is smooth, and His clear eyes tell us the kindness and love of His character. He is an attractive man, someone we want to be with. As we look at images of this Jesus, our hearts are warmed.

It is all so nice and tidy, but there is one glitch. The Scripture does not so depict Him:

> For He shall grow up before Him as a tender plant,
> And as a root out of dry ground.
> He has no form or comeliness;
> And when we see Him,
> [There] [is] no beauty that we should desire Him.
> He is despised and rejected by men,
> A Man of sorrows and acquainted with grief.
> And we hid, as it were, [our] faces from Him;
> He was despised, and we did not esteem Him.
>
> Isaiah 53:2–3 (NKJV)

He had "no beauty that we should desire Him." According to God's own words, Jesus was not much to look at.

> "Is this not the carpenter, the Son of Mary, and brother of James, Joses, Judas, and Simon? And are not His sisters here with us?" And they were offended at Him.
>
> Mark 6:3 (NKJV)

Of His four earthly brothers, He would not have been the pick of the litter. And as to His modern image, it is highly unlikely that he had long hair. Among the Jews only the Nazirites such as Samson vowed not to cut their hair, drink wine, or come near a dead body. Jesus drank wine prior to His resurrection and touched the dead as he raised them, so He clearly did not take these vows. (Jesus was from Nazareth and was called a Nazarene, Jesus of Nazareth, but was not a Nazirite. The words are similar but they aren't the same.)

Try as we might, we want to follow appearances. We are still, like the Pharisees, washing the outside of the cup.[24] What is inside is of lesser consequence to us. We have painted God's Son to our liking and for our comfort. We do not measure as God measures.

> For the Lord does not see as man sees; for man looks at the outward appearance, but the Lord looks at the heart.
>
> 1 Samuel 16:7b (NKJV)

Would we have accepted Jesus had we lived when He walked the earth? We like to think so. We like to think our hearts not as hard as many of the Jews of the day. But truth be known, we see a different Jesus than they saw. Faced with the Jesus of Scripture, what would we have thought, what gossipy statements would have entered our hearts, and what would we have really believed ?

---

[24]   Matthew 23:25

This is Jesus is kind, courageous, caring, and strong. Can you follow Him? Can you love Him?

If you find yourself too influenced by appearances, welcome to a large club. Even so, don't feel guilty. The grace of God overwhelms our frailty. To brood over our shortcomings is to add selfishness to an already full list. Instead, focus on two things.

First, accept that our depiction of Christ is simply wrong. Decide to pull away from the man-made image and believe what God has said. Some may find it difficult to sever ties with a picture on the wall that gives warm feelings for our Savior. They may ask, "What could be wrong with a constant reminder of the kindness and love of Jesus even if the face isn't historically correct?"

Frankly, I don't know. What I do know is that God's truth is best for us regardless of our inability to understand why. And God's truth is that we serve a plain-faced, homely Christ. He could have been good-looking if the Father had so desired. We must conclude that He had a reason, and that is the wonder and the depth of God. So our second task is simply to believe.

It is never a waste of time to inquire about what God has said and why He has said it. We don't have to look far to guess at what it was. From Isaiah 53, we know directly that His looks were meant to discourage any desire for Him based on appearance. The Pharisees were fond of splendid attire, of the outward appearance. They serve us as a great contrast to Jesus and what was most important to Him. Could it be that His lack of beauty itself made a statement? He did not want to personify that which He detested in the Pharisees. He was all about the spirit and not the flesh. Real belief had to look beyond appearance. Allow that truth to focus you on the greater prize of His character, His words, His deeds, and His holiness.

Inner beauty is exactly what smacked me in the face the Sunday that I judged the woman in the choir. After the opening song, she was lead singer. I had never heard her voice stand out from all the rest. I have rarely heard such beautiful tones. I cannot begin to describe the clarity and almost angelic pureness of sound. God had given her a wonderful instrument, and she could make it do and go wherever she needed it. As I stood there, I could no longer sing. The water welled up in my eyes and my throat tightened as the power of her voice and words lifted me to the Savior:

> And As I wait I'll rise up like an eagle.
> And I will soar with You
> Your spirit leads me on
> In the power of Your love[25]

I no longer had to ask, "Why was she there?" I was doubly and triply ashamed, yet so impressed with the love of God that the thrill of worship overshadowed my guilt. I no longer had to fight against judging the outside of this woman as she had helped the spirit fill me inside. My crooked mind turned off because my heart had been turned on.

If you are still having a hard time with the ugly Jesus, please cheer up. The time of His homeliness is over. His inward character now shines through to uncontrollable glory. He has a beauty that makes our good-looking guy pictures quite sorry indeed. How horrible these pictures must seem to the messengers who worship before the throne and see the glory of God radiant in the face of Jesus.[26]

---

[25]   Geoff Bullock, "The Power of Your Love"
[26]   II Corinthians 4:6

To love the Lord our God[27] is our first and greatest commandment. Yet it is not enough. The second[28] asks that we love one another. It seems even more difficult since we can be a bit ugly on the inside as well as the outside. It helps to know that one day, in the twinkle of an eye, the spirit that lives within us will shine without.

Yet the questions remain. Can I love a homely Savior; can I love the least of these?[29]

Reflections

1. Have you ever loved someone who was physically unattractive? How?
2. Have you ever kept your distance because someone looked broken or unsightly?
3. How could you apply your experience of loving in the first question to people you may have backed away from in the second?
4. According to Scripture, what is the difference between how man sees and the Lord sees?

---

[27]   Matthew 22:37
[28]   Matthew 22:39
[29]   Matthew 25:40

After Death: Is Heaven Instant?

I had made my way down the hall and into my office when at around 8:30 a.m. someone asked me if I had seen David Lee, a member of our Information Technology team. There was concern in the question. Come to think of it, I hadn't. He hadn't been in his office when I went by. No one had seen him. No show and no call. This wasn't like David.

Common Belief

Death sends us instantly to the Lord.

He had joined our family-owned company only a year before to answer the myriad of computer and software questions we, non-technical types get stuck on. He always met each person with a positive and calm approach and was immediately accepted as part of the family.

David had arrived as a single, young man with a quiet integrity and, as it happened, with no friends or family in Denver. The friends he found at work truly became his family. It was no surprise that when he rekindled his relationship with Cami and they began to get serious about marriage, he brought her in from

Salt Lake City to meet the family. David and Cami were soon married, and Cami came to Denver, likewise without family other than her new husband and her friends at Sashco. She was easy to adopt. Everyone was thrilled to see David and Cami move into a new house and start life together.

That particular morning, we were wondering why we hadn't heard from David. By 9 a.m., the call came in that he had been in a severe auto accident just one and a half blocks from work. His friends at work rallied quickly and went to the hospital to be with Cami, but they discovered she was there only to identify him. David had died at the scene. The bride of four months was instantly, tragically, and unexplainably a young widow. The young man we admired and depended upon no longer sat at his desk, as though on extended vacation from which there would be no return.

Each time we face the death of someone close we are struck with hard reality. There are no guarantees. Not for ourselves, not for those beside us. One day, a man is alive and vital, and the next, he is a lifeless shell. What can help us? What can encourage us? How can we be consoled when facing the ultimate pain of loss?

We who believe that God through Christ can and will raise those of faith to immortality have a hope. And with that hope, we are to console one another. If there is no resurrection of the dead, says the Apostle Paul, then we are more forlorn and more forsaken than all men.[30] In that case, we Christians live a fairy-tale existence, while those who believe only in life on earth deal with reality.

But we do not live a fairy-tale existence if Christ has conquered death both for Himself and for us. And we do console one another as we must when death has called. Despite our hope and our faith, death bites deep and stings hard. Loved ones are gone. For those of us left behind, relationship is suddenly and completely cut off. We cannot wake up tomorrow and have that

---

[30]   I Corinthians 15:19

last discussion. We cannot say the I love yous, the I'm sorrys, or the please forgive mes.

It is not surprising how strong our urge is to console and to be consoled. Some without faith in Christ seek mediums to have that last discussion with the dead. Theirs is a hope that hopes the dead are not really dead, that they are somehow still alive, still accessible. Christians tell each other that their loved ones are instantly in another place, a better place. The pain of earthly and fleshly existence is gone. Your aunt, your mother, your spouse is now with Christ—happy, filled with joy, not shackled with pain. She may even be looking down on you now with kind and understanding eyes. Despite the loss you suffer, at least she is in heaven communing with the Lord. And it is with these words we console ourselves.

The need for consolation is not wrong. We are not expected to rejoice, as those in heaven do,[31] at the death of a saint. Jesus wept at the sorrow of Lazarus's passing though He knew He was to raise Lazarus from the dead. The emotion of the moment does not escape our Lord. It is further comfort that the Apostle Paul encourages us to consolation:

> For this we are saying to you by the word of the Lord, that we, the living, who are surviving to the presence of the Lord, should by no means outstrip those who are put to repose, for the Lord Himself will be descending from heaven with a shout of command, with the voice of the Chief messenger, and with the trumpet of God, and the dead in Christ shall be rising first, Thereupon we, the living who are surviving, shall at the same time be snatched away together with them in clouds, to meet the Lord in the air. And thus shall we always be together with the Lord. So that, console one another with *these words.*
>
> 1 Thessalonians 4:15–18 (CLV); italics added

---

[31] Psalm 116:15

The essentials are that the Lord will descend from heaven with a shout, the dead in Christ shall rise first, and those who are alive at His coming will rise after them and meet the Lord in the air. Notice that there is a definite sequence. Those saints who have died will rise first. Thereafter, those who have not experienced death will be changed and join the Lord as well.[32]

Now let us think about these, the clear words of Scripture. We are to console one another based upon the return of Christ. Yes, your loved ones are dead, but they shall be resurrected. But like Lazarus,[33] they must wait upon the Lord. Nothing in these words consoles us concerning what happens to loved ones at the very time of death. According to this Scripture, consolation comes when Jesus comes and not before. But these are not the words we use for consolation. We say that our loved ones are now with Christ—right now, conscious and happy in their new place.

If that is true, why has the Scripture left these words of consolation out? Nowhere does Paul say, "Console one another that your loved one is with Christ." What he does say is that the dead in Christ shall be rising first, so that console one another with these words. Is this a mistake? Doesn't the Lord get it? Or have we added our own spin? Maybe it's not the way we think it is.

Let's face it that if our concept of instant resurrection were true, this would have been a great time for the apostle to tell us. Why didn't he? Why is the pinnacle consolation, in fact the only consolation prescribed by Scripture totally dependent upon the return of Christ?

Doesn't the Lord get it?

Rethinking the subject of death and resurrection may be some rough ground for even the most objective person. Perhaps, you have consoled another or even been consoled yourself by thoughts of a loved one instantly transported

---

[32]   I Corinthians 15:52
[33]   John 11:6

to heaven. This way of thinking and feeling is so ingrained it is almost reflex habit. It may be an emotional strain, but we need to put it aside and take a fresh look. Yet if we have layered on extra content to God's truth, then stripping it away should hold no fear. His truth is always to our benefit.

Resurrection: What's the Point?

The common notion that we go immediately to be with the Lord when we die forces us to face a basic question: what is the point of resurrection? In other words, we would already be alive and up in heaven, so why bother with a resurrection yet to come? What do we call this first transfer to the Lord? It isn't the bodily resurrection mentioned in Thessalonians, so what is it? Where else is it mentioned in Scripture?

By saying that we immediately rise up to the Lord, we are really putting forth the idea that the resurrection of the dead has already happened. Are we participating in an error that the Apostle Paul warned about even in his day?

> Who concerning the truth have erred, saying that the resurrection is past already; and overthrow the faith of some.
>
> 2 Timothy 2:18 (KJV)

When Lazarus died, Martha did not console herself that he was already experiencing heaven in spirit. Jesus consoled her with the future resurrection.

> Jesus said to her, "Your brother will rise again." Martha said to Him, "I know that he will rise again in the resurrection at the last day."
>
> John 11:23–24 (NKJV)

Martha understood her hope and Jesus did not contradict her. She did not talk about how Lazarus was with God now and looking down fondly on her and her sister. Her expectation was the eventual resurrection her brother would experience was not now but at the last day. What she didn't know was that Lazarus would experience a foretaste of what Jesus will do on the last day.

If Lazarus had already gone to heaven, then he would have been pretty ticked off. He would have died in faith, tasted of heaven, seen perfection, and been brought back in stinky wrappings.[34] Everyone else might have been rejoicing, but Lazarus wouldn't have been that pleased. He was among the very few that were to die twice. "I am present with God; please don't bother me." In fact, we are not told what his reaction was, but you get the point. It raises a very practical question as to what resurrection is all about. If we go instantly and consciously to heaven upon death, then the event of resurrection is an afterthought, a non-event.

But it isn't a non-event, and we, like Lazarus, must wait upon the Lord. That is a point of faith. That is what we anxiously await because it is our gateway to life with Christ. That is why we should console one another with His return. Instead, we have shifted the words of Scripture to grab early delivery and early consolation, minimizing His return in power and His shout of command to a mere administrative chore. Remember, it was He Who spoke creation into existence, that through Christ, God's words have life-giving power. I believe that He will call the saints by name as He did with Lazarus. "Lazarus! Hither! Out!"[35] The trumpet of the messenger will sound, and He will shout, "Rise!" and the dead in Christ shall rise. If we are so lucky as to be living, what a consuming scene we will observe. In the midst of a miracle, in the power of the Son of God, we will hear the joyful sound of our loved one's names, "Arise, _____!" We will see thousands of saints escape the grave, and we (who are alive) will go with them to meet the Lord in the air.

---

[34]   John 11:17, 11:39
[35]   John 11:43

What a tender mercy it is that the Lord raises those who died first and those who are alive at the time second, not forgetting them nor being tardy as to His promise. We dampen that moment by believing that they are with the Lord already. That is like seeing the end of the movie first and then being asked to get all excited about watching the middle.

We Grasp for a Reason for Later Resurrection

Since there isn't a good reason for resurrection if we are already with the Lord, we grasp for one. And what our traditional thinking asks us to believe is that although we are with the Lord, we don't have our new bodies yet. So we are really alive and communing with the Lord, but our spiritual body is still in the shop. And we long to be clothed[36] in it, and that is what resurrection is really about. This thinking implies that we are in heaven with the Lord, but we are not quite complete. We may await judgment, and we still don't have new bodies. In fact, we have no body at all as our old ones were left behind. If this is true, some saints have been waiting over 2000 years to be clothed in their new bodies.

This just isn't plausible. The picture of millions of people residing in heaven not quite perfected, marking time while awaiting their new bodies, having to return to earth to go get them, stretches the imagination. What can't they do? They don't have their new bodies. They must need it for something or God would not have it in reserve. The new spiritual bodies[37] we wait for allow us to perform like Christ, yet what could we perform without them?

> For our realm is inherent in the heavens, out of which we are awaiting a Saviour also, the Lord, Jesus Christ, Who will transfigure the body of our humiliation, to conform

---

[36]   II Corinthians 5:2
[37]   I Corinthians 15:45

it to the body of His glory, in accord with the operation
which enables Him even to subject all to Himself.

Philippians 3:20–21 (CLV)

Our Savior comes out of the heavens, and we are waiting for
Him. Why, if we are already with Him, would we await Him out
of heaven? I have never told my wife that I would wait for her
to come home if she was already there. Isn't it plain that when
Christ descends from heaven, we are resurrected, and then we get
our spiritual bodies that enable us to reside in heaven?

Sleep, the Picture of Death

What is death after all? Is death another form of life? When we
discover what Scripture says about death, will it match the instant
heaven model or will it match the future resurrection model?

Consider [and] hear me, O LORD my God: lighten mine
eyes, lest I sleep the [sleep of] death;

Psalm 13:3 (KJV)

The Scripture uses the analogy of sleep quite often to explain
the death state. Jesus used it Himself.

He [Jesus] is saying to them, "Lazarus, our friend, has
found repose, but I am going that I should be awakening
him out of sleep." The disciples, then, said to Him, "Lord,
if he has repose, he shall be saved." Now Jesus had made a
declaration concerning his death, yet they suppose that He
is saying it concerning the repose of sleep. Jesus, then, said
to them with boldness then "Lazarus died."

John 11:11–14 (CLV)

What is it about sleep that is analogous to death? Have you
ever wondered why we sleep or need sleep? When you're tired,
nothing sounds better. But we are a bit too close to it to objectively
stand back and really wonder at it. My son, Jeff, pointed out to me

the strangeness of sleep—that there is something spiritual going on here. It really is a weird kind of experience. We put ourselves in a kind of trance. Do you know it takes the average person only seven minutes to fall asleep? We just lie down and shut down. It reminds me of C-3PO, the Star Wars robot, who announces he has to shut down, and he actually pushes the button himself. It's funny in the movie because we can see how strange our practices are when performed by a robot. How is it that we shut down? We don't control going to sleep and neither do we quite control coming out of it. Many who can't sleep wish they could.

Yet through all the mystery of sleep, why does it exist at all? Could it be to teach us the difference between life and death? When we go into a very good sleep, a sound and undisturbed sleep, time passes without notice. One minute, your head is lying down on the pillow and the next moment, the sun is peaking through the window. Unless we dream, we just don't have a sense of time passing or a sense of being conscious through the night.

What is death like? How far does the sleep analogy go? How much like sleep is death? A valuable picture of death can be built by noting what Scripture says about death, and why it compares it to sleep. No doubt, it uses sleep because it is something we know about.

> For the living know that they shall die,
> But the dead know nothing whatsoever;
> There is no further reward for them;
> Indeed remembrance of them is forgotten.
> Both their love and their hate as well as their jealousy have
> perished already,
> And there is no further portion for them for the eon
> In all that is done under the sun.
>
> Ecclesiastes 9:5–6 (CLV)

This passage allows us to draw many comparisons to sleep. The living people know that they shall die, but the dead know nothing:

they have no relationship with others and they aren't doing anything—no work, no play. When we are asleep we are about as useless as the dead on all counts. We can build a list of the characteristics of sleep that relate to death.

The dead cannot praise God

- We are not conscious.
- We are not aware of time.
- We have little control of going into or out of sleep.
- We do not communicate or relate to others.
- We do not get any work done.

Did you know that the dead cannot praise God?

> The dead cannot praise Yah,
> Nor all those descending into stillness.
> But we, we the living, shall bless Yah,
> Henceforth and unto the eon.
> Praise Yah!
>
> Psalm 115:17–18 (CLV)

The dead, because they have descended into stillness, do not talk to God; they don't talk to each other; and they don't talk to the living.

> For in death [there is] no remembrance of thee: in the grave who shall give thee thanks?
>
> Psalm 6:5 (KJV)

> Wilt thou shew wonders to the dead? Shall the dead arise [and] praise thee? Selah. Shall thy lovingkindness be declared in the grave? [or] thy faithfulness in destruction? Shall thy wonders be known in the dark? and thy righteousness in the land of forgetfulness?
>
> Psalm 88:10–12 (KJV)

They are in the land of forgetfulness. Not that God has forgotten them and not that those yet alive have forgotten them. But they themselves have no memory. If you were to go to be with the Lord as soon as you die, you could indeed praise the Lord. But the Psalms are especially stubborn on this point. "The dead cannot praise Yah"

Death is death and life is life. Death is not a different consciousness. Even King David and the faithful patriarchs are still in their tombs awaiting the resurrection.

> "Men! Brethren! Allow me to say to you with boldness concerning the patriarch David, that he deceases also and was entombed, and his tomb is among us until this day.
>
> Acts 2:29 (CLV)

David, like Joshua before him,[38] went the way of all the earth. Dust to dust. To proclaim that death is another form of life (they are now with the Lord) is to agree with Satan's lie: "You shall not surely die."[39] But they surely did die. It shouldn't surprise us that Satan is still drawing people away with his first lie. Do we believe he has stopped telling it? Do we believe that Adam and Eve were the only ones susceptible? When he whispered in their ear, "You shall not surely die," he convinced them that God doesn't really mean what He says. When he whispers in our ears that death isn't really death, he convinces us that there is no need to hope in the return of Christ. Man must not live on the whispers of the Adversary but on every word from the mouth of God.

> This, also, do, being aware of the era, that it is already the hour for us to be roused out of sleep, for now is our salvation nearer than when we believe.
>
> Romans 13:11 (CLV)

---

[38]   Joshua 23:14
[39]   Genesis 3:4

What About Our Spirit?

But doesn't something happen with our spirit? This whole issue of death is about more than our physical bodies, isn't it? Yes, the Scripture is quite clear about that. We do not cease to exist.

> Then shall the dust return to the earth as it was: and the spirit shall return unto God who gave it.
>
> Ecclesiastes 12:7 (KJV)

What was put together, the spirit with the body to form a living soul[40] is taken back apart. From dust we were made and to dust we return. God gave us each a spirit, and He takes it back. How conscious were we before our births? If we were, we certainly have no memory of it. Yet God had our spirits with Him as our gift of life. Who we are and who we were is taken back and stored by God. But it doesn't mean we are conscious. If we were, we could praise God and death would not be the land of forgetfulness.

But What About?

I know what you're thinking. Aren't there some verses that picture a conscious life right after death? Isn't there a passage that does imply that we are either alive on earth or alive with the Lord? Before we look at the specifics, we should consider the broad implications of any verse that might imply that we go instantly to heaven. If that verse exists, would it cause you to say, "Aha! I knew I was right, and this guy is off base"? Or would you realize instead that if that verse exists, it would be in conflict with the verses we have looked at so far, especially the New Testament passage that puts our consolation in a future resurrection[41] and not in an instant pass to heaven? Would you be tempted to rely on the one verse

Is it what I want to believe?

---

40   Genesis 2:7
41   I Thessalonians 4:18

that supports your belief and ignore the many others that contradict it? Searching for the truth of Scripture is not a matter of debate, of who is right and who is wrong. If you want to believe something, you can usually grab a verse to support it even if the idea is contradicted by other passages. All of us are guilty at one time or another of holding onto our comfortable conclusions, not wanting to be bothered with troublesome facts, as if by hiding our heads in the sand we can make it true for us. That is when we must gird our loins with the renewed faith that Scripture is not in conflict with itself, and it is our lifelong job to understand how passages that seem in conflict with one another are all, nevertheless, true.

"To be absent from the body is to be present with the Lord." Is that the verse you were thinking of? Seems clear enough; you are either in the body or with the Lord. No in-between. Read the verse carefully in the larger context.

> So [we] [are] always confident, knowing that while we are at home in the body we are absent from the Lord. For we walk by faith, not by sight. We are confident, yes, well pleased rather to be absent from the body and to be present with the Lord. Therefore we make it our aim, whether present or absent, to be well pleasing to Him. For we must all appear before the judgment seat of Christ, that each one may receive the things [done] in the body, according to what he has done, whether good or bad.
>
> 2 Corinthians 5:6–10 (NKJV)

I hope you noticed that this passage doesn't say what we think it says. It doesn't say to be absent *is* to be present. The phrase is familiar but misquoted. The verse talks instead about two states of life: one here in our fleshly body and one that is present with the Lord. This verse really doesn't deal with death or the process of how we get to be present with the Lord. The hard fact is that as long as we are in this body we cannot be present with the Lord.

We are used to holding on tightly to this existence since the life ahead is unknown. It takes a lot of faith to be excited to leave here. In fact, if we were truly enthralled to get there so quickly, we would all commit suicide. It would be the rational thing to do. Yet the apostle says that we are encouraged or confident or willing to be absent from this body and present with the Lord. He is trying to bolster our faith and confidence that leaving this body is a good thing because our next life with the Lord is much better than this one. Take encouragement. Be confident in the life to come.

None of this speaks of death. The passage makes no statement that being absent from the body instantly and automatically makes us at home with the Lord. The process by which we get to the next life is left out. The apostle is emphasizing the development of confidence in life with Christ.

The Rich Man and Lazarus

What about the famous story of the rich man and the poor fellow named Lazarus (not the brother of Mary and Martha), who both died and end up having a lively discussion with, of all people, Abraham?[42] Since the images and information in this passage are extensive, we will focus only on our current question of whether it depicts death and destiny in quite a different way from other parts of Scripture, realizing that if it does we have a problem to solve.

---

[42]   Luke 16:19-31

Verses Relating to Death	The Rich Man and the Poor Man
What man can live and not see death? Can he deliver his life [soul] from the power of the grave? Selah **Psalm 89:48 (NKJV)**	"So it was that the beggar died, and was carried by the angels to Abraham's bosom. The rich man also died and was buried." **Luke 16:22 (NKJV)**
For dust you [are], And to dust you shall return. **Genesis 3:19b (NKJV)**	23 "And being in torments in Hades, he lifted up his eyes and saw Abraham afar off, and Lazarus in his bosom.
For as the body without the spirit is dead, so faith without works is dead also. **James 2:26 (NKJV)**	
Let the wicked be ashamed; Let them be silent in the grave. **Psalm 31:17b (NKJV)** The dead cannot praise Yah, Nor all those descending into stillness. **Psalm 115:17 (CLV)**	24 "Then he cried and said, 'Father Abraham, have mercy on me, and send Lazarus that he may dip the tip of his finger in water and cool my tongue; for I am tormented in this flame.' 25 "But Abraham said, 'Son, remember that in your lifetime you received your good things, and likewise Lazarus evil things; but now he is comforted and you are tormented. 31 "But he said to him, 'If they do not hear Moses and the prophets, neither will they be persuaded though one rise from the dead.' "

The souls of all of the dead (the word *life* in Psalm 89 is *soul*) go to the grave (or Sheol), yet the poor man in the story ends up in Abraham's bosom. The rich man lifted up his eyes and saw Abraham, yet the body is said to decay and return to the dust. When death occurs, the spirit leaves the body, according to James, and the body is dead. How then does the rich man still have a body with functioning eyes to see and mouth to talk and ears to hear? The dead cannot praise the Lord, and there is silence and stillness in the grave, yet the rich man has a long, drawn-out conversation with Abraham. If this is literal, then heaven must be in very close proximity to the grave or the pit since all parties can see each other.

The verses on the left contradict those on the right at every turn. So what are we to do? If Scripture is right, then both of these must make sense. I will suggest a possible solution, yet nothing near a complete study.

If we press the idea that this story is the true picture of death for the saved versus the unsaved, that it is the literal destiny of mankind, then we should be able to test the literal sense of the parts presented and how they correlate to other things we know. The poor man is carried by angels into Abraham's bosom. What is Abraham's bosom? Can we take this literally? How big is his bosom, and how many folks can fit in? Of course, this must be figurative, but even so, what other Scripture can we find that describes heaven as figuratively being in Abraham's bosom? We await a Savior out of heaven who will take us into heaven, yet the poor man is carried away by angels. How does this correlate?

The poor man is with Abraham, and the rich man is in the grave. If this prescribes literal destiny, then it teaches that salvation is brought only to the poor, while the rich end in torment. If you got good things in this life you will have pain in death, and if you were shortchanged on earth you go to Abraham's bosom. This definitely sounds like works salvation. We can see that the rich man did not come to the aid of the poor and, thus, his painful destiny. However, we see nothing in the actions of the poor man deserving of a place with Abraham. He is just poor. For those of the body of Christ who believe in salvation by faith, how can this passage that teaches salvation by "poordom" be used as the guide for death and destiny? It is shaky ground indeed.

The rich man pleads with Abraham to allow him to return to his living brothers and warn them of a painful destiny. Abraham denies his request. Where else do we learn of Abraham being the judge of the dead, the one who arbitrates destiny? Will Abraham be our judge? If this is literal, there ought to be a whole doctrine around being accepted by Abraham. Is Abraham alive today, or did he die, return to his dust, and now awaits the resurrection into the kingdom of promise?

Rather than deny the truths about death found in so many other passages, I would suggest that the story of the rich man and the helpless poor man, Lazarus, is a parable just as the stories that precede it. Some have pointed out that the Scripture does not specifically name it as a parable. Of the four preceding stories, which most everyone agrees are parables—the lost sheep, the lost coin, the prodigal son, and the unjust steward—only the first one, the lost sheep, is introduced by "Now He told them this parable. . ."[43] It is probable that all five are one extended parable from Luke 15:3 to 16:31. It is symbolic of things pertaining especially to the destiny of Israel, with Father Abraham symbolic of their physical claim to the holy nation, but it is not a literal picture of death.

Unraveling the symbolism of the parables is a study of its own and not the key issue here. What is most important is not whether the contradictions are solved by seeing the story as a parable but that there are contradictions and they do need to be solved. How would you solve this puzzle?

Aren't We Conformed to His Death?

Some may protest that Christ's example is the pattern for us. He, after all, went to minister in spirit to the spirits in jail[44] prior to His own bodily resurrection. Quite true. Yet where do we read that this is for us? Christ also spoke creation into existence, walked through walls and on water, changed forms, appeared across the sea without walking there, commanded the wind, controlled evil spirits, turned water into wine, raised the dead, and showed His glory—all this before His resurrection! We cannot compare our death as if we will mimic the three days before His resurrection. His flesh did not decay nor was He forsaken in Hades (the grave). We will conform to His death only in that we will be resurrected to immortal life.[45] We are not told that we will follow the patterns that He walked. We are not Him. We are not encouraged to console one another by saying that our flesh is not decaying or that our spirit is now ministering to the underworld or looking

---

[43]   Luke 15:3

[44]   I Peter 3:19

[45]   Philippians 3:10

down upon the living on the earth. If it were so, He would have told us.

Who Is in Heaven?

If the dead in Christ access heaven instantly, there would be thousands, perhaps millions, of believers already in heaven. How would you measure that up against this verse?

> No one has ascended to heaven but He who came down from heaven, [that] [is], the Son of Man who is in heaven.
>
> John 3:13 (NKJV)

"No one has ascended to heaven but He . . ." John wrote this after Christ's death, resurrection, and ascension to the Father. Certainly, there were believers who died before John wrote, yet none had ascended into heaven, and we have no reason to believe that has changed. If our familiar passage in Corinthians really said that "to be absent from the body *is* to be present with the Lord," it would be in direct conflict with this verse in John. Luckily, it doesn't say that, and we can firmly believe that we wait for our Savior out of the heavens because He is the only one Who has ascended to heaven.[46] Since no one of humanity has yet ascended, there is every reason to believe that we need the new body provided by the coming resurrection to be fit to join the Lord in the air.

Our Consolation or God's?

Paul needed to tell the Thessalonians (and us) how this resurrection thing works. We can't know it by intuition. And he tells us chiefly for our consolation, not just so we know the program.

> For this we are saying to you by the word of the Lord, that we, the living, who are surviving to the presence of

---

[46] Philippians 3:20

the Lord, should by no means outstrip those who are put to repose.

1 Thessalonians 4:15 (CLV)

His statement in this verse is interesting. "We who are surviving should by no means *outstrip* those who are put to repose." Other translations have *precede*. Paul wants us to know that those who live to the presence of the Lord will have no advantage over those who have died. We do not get there sooner; we are not better off than they.

Why would we think that we, the living, would be better off? Well, because we who are alive at the time pass from life to death to life in the "blink of an eye."[47] We shed our old bodies and pick up our new ones instantly. Paul is concerned that some might think that the living are with Christ sooner than the dead. But, he assures us,

> The dead in Christ shall be rising first, Thereupon we, the living who are surviving...

1 Thessalonians 4:16b, 17a (CLV)

If we follow the popular thought that those who die go immediately to the Lord in a conscious way, then they—the dead—are much better off than the living. The dead, in that case, would already be with Christ ahead of the living. But the apostle consoles us that the living have no advantage over those that sleep! People of the day understood that you aren't alive and conscious until you are resurrected and that the dead know nothing.[48]

God has not forgotten our loved ones who have died. He has taken their spirits back until the day resurrection comes. He knows each of them intimately. He knows them by name. In that day, they will awaken from their sleep as if no time has

---

[47]   I Corinthians 15:52
[48]   Ecclesiastes 9:5

passed. And that is a great mercy. To them 1,000 years will be as a brief moment.

To deal squarely with what death means can be a frightening thought. We are literally dismantled, the body to dust, the soul to the grave, and the spirit to God. There is absolutely nothing we can do about it. When you are dead you are dead. Like the seed that must die and lie dormant[49] until the warmth of the spring rains awaken it, so we must wait upon the sound of the trumpet and His command to awaken. The mystery and the faith of it all is that we are like Lazarus: totally helpless, unaware, and unable to raise ourselves. The name *Lazarus* means helpless, and we are lazarus. What can put us together again? All the king's horses and all the king's men cannot do it. We need encouraging words. We need the consolation of Christ's return. We need resurrection.

The gracious gift of God is life.[50] He has given us great words of consolation that promise the glorious life-giving return of Christ. We are not without hope as those who do not know Him. We are not to use our own words and ideas as if His are second best.

When you are dead, you are dead

> Behold, I tell you a mystery: We shall not all sleep, but we shall all be changed—in a moment, in the twinkling of an eye, at the last trumpet. For the trumpet will sound, and the dead will be raised incorruptible, and we shall be changed.
>
> 1 Corinthians 15:51–52 (NKJV)

When we die, we do not quietly slip away to heaven, check out our robe, get our chair assignment, and begin peering down on the earth as if we had nothing better to do, all without a body. When we take an unbiblical view of death, as some form of in-between life,

---

[49]   John 12:24
[50]   Romans 6:23

we diminish the moment of our change, as though methodically in a slow march over the decades and centuries, accepting bit-by-bit the adversary's deception, "You shall not surely die." We have dulled the gleaming steel of the sword of His word[51] into a blunt club that strikes with an anticlimactic thud, leaving no cause for the great musical fanfare foretold. We can't allow it.

Our awakening to incorruptible, immortal life is a magnificent event announced by the clear and resounding blast of His trumpet. What believer will not thrill at the sound, and feel the great power of Christ unlocking the graves of every single person who has died in Christ? Have you felt the electricity of a stadium crowd 75,000 strong, cheering their team in the final playoff moment? It can be exhilarating. But it cannot compare to the resurrection scene.

The entire earth is the stadium, millions rising in one thunderous and joyous moment to meet the Lord in the air. And you will not be a spectator. You will be in the game, on the field, winning the prize. You will be changed, and you will meet the Lord. And thus, you shall always be together with the Lord.

"So that, console one another with *these* words."[52]

Reflections

1. When someone dies, what do you believe happens with the body, spirit, and soul? What Scriptures would you use to support that belief?

2. Do you think that believers who have died are in heaven now? How much of your belief is influenced by what you prefer to believe and how much by Scripture?

3. What are some advantages of believing that we sleep until Christ comes?

---

[51]   Hebrews 4:12

[52]   I Thessalonians 4:18

The Trinity—
Help or Hindrance?

When you finish this chapter, you will have a fresh look, a deeper look, a more startling and earthy look at the Son of God than ever before. He did more than our heart of hearts can give credit for. And it impacts us and it unmasks us and it makes our sin worse and our rescue the more unimaginable. What I am saying is that we have missed the real Jesus. Oh, we know about His sacrifice for our sins, but we gloss over the everyday step-by-courageous-step of His life without sin. It's not our fault.

> **Common Belief**
>
> *The trinity correctly describes our God as existing in three parts, and it is heresy to question it.*

Not all of it. We've been shackled and hamstrung and lead down a path so blurred we can't hope to see the detail. The path I'm talking about is the concept of the trinity. From theologian to religious bystander, everyone knows and everyone admits that they don't understand it. It is too mysterious, too complex, too wrapped up in the depths of godness to be grasped. This is the murkiness we deal with in our attempt to understand God. What if the concept of the trinity is just that, a concept and not a fact? What if this idea we can't explain, this notion we've passively given a head nod, does more to obscure than explain? What if there is more to God and His Son than we ever thought possible? What if it isn't the way we think it is?

Part 1 Decoding Trinity

Do you understand the trinity? Can you explain it with conviction to someone else? Have you used the trinity as central in helping believers to deeper God knowledge or drawing the open-hearted to salvation? If your answers are "not really," "I don't think so," or "no, I haven't," then this chapter will help.

The concept of the trinity that is used to explain the relation between God, His Son, and the Holy Spirit should be clear and convincing. It should be usable to expand our love and appreciation for God and for His Son. It should augment our understanding and thrill our hearts.

But we are ahead of ourselves. The most important issue is what you believe, how clear the concept is in your mind, and how you would typically explain it. Taking a little time to write down where your thinking is will help you decode the trinity as you go through this chapter. Please explain the trinity as you might to any newcomer. Feel free to use extra paper if you need more room.

Did you have any problems? Is your description clear and concise? Does it flow from the understandings gained from Scripture? When constructing your explanation, what terms or phrases did you use? Any of the following sound familiar: Godhead, God in three persons, the three are one, second person of the trinity, fully God and fully man, God the Son, God the Holy Spirit, Jesus is God?

If you struggled a bit, don't worry. You seem to be in good company. Throughout many centuries, none have claimed to understand it despite the many analogies conjured up to explain it. I have never read a theologian who did not say that it is difficult to understand and even mysterious. Here is a typical explanation from a theological internet page:

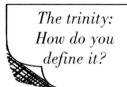

The trinity: How do you define it?

> One of the most often misunderstood beliefs that Christians hold is the idea of the trinity. Christians often find themselves at a loss as to how to adequately express their understanding (and many times simply express an incorrect view). This summary should help. There are two platforms that must be understood to grasp the true essence of this teaching:
>
> 1. There is only one God (not three).
> 2. God exists in three distinct persons (not one).
>
> God is one in nature (there is only one what), and three in person (there are three whos). Because we only find one person per essence in humanity, this is hard to understand! But an infinite essence can certainly be shared by three persons.[53]

---

[53]   Doug Beaumont, "The Trinity," http://www.souldevice.org/christian_trinity.html (accessed March 2006).]

Fact is, it's confusing, so don't feel bad. We are told that we don't understand it but do and must believe it. Do you feel good about believing something you can't explain?[54]

Here is another attempt by James M. Arlandson.

> This doctrine teaches that God exists in three persons who share the same essence or being. What this means is that God exists in the distinct and coequal persons of the Father, the Son, and the Holy Spirit, but they share a fully divine essence or being, such as uncreatedness, eternality, simplicity (non-composite or indivisible), immutability (unchangeableness), omniscience (all-wise and knowing), omnipotence (all-powerful), goodness, mercy, holiness, will and freedom, and so on.
>
> Thus, in God, the attributes of his essence are fully shared by three persons, making each person fully God. Yet, the three persons are distinct. The Father is neither the Son nor the Holy Spirit; the Son is neither the Father nor the Holy Spirit; and the Holy Spirit is neither the Father nor the Son.[55]

I get it. They are the same but they are different. They are three but they are one. There is one what and three whos. I don't know about you but these explanations don't help much. So difficult is the struggle to grasp this concept that people have made up several analogies to try to explain it.

Perhaps you used some of the popular analogies. The trinity is like:

- An egg (shell, white, and yolk)

---

[54] But aren't there things about God we *can't* understand? See note i under this chapter in the end notes.

[55] James M Arlandson, "A Brief Explanation of The Trinity," http://answering-islam.org.uk/Authors/Arlandson/trinity_brief.htm (accessed March 18, 2006).

- A triangle (3 points but just one triangle)
- Love (a lover, the loved, and the spirit between)
- Water (solid, liquid, and gas)
- A chain of 3 links
- 3 in 1 or the 3 are 1
- 1x1x1=1 (this is supposed to fix the 3 are 1 analogy since 1+1+1 equals 3 but is supposed to equal 1)
- Infinity x Infinity x Infinity (I really don't know what this equals.)

Those attempting to explain the trinity concept argue over which, if any, of these analogies really hold up. The point is not which is the best but simply to show the ongoing and ever deepening confusion surrounding the whole subject.

The analogies are no help

The more we use the trinity to explain God, the more confused we become. It has caused disunity within the church and has not built the "unity of the spirit with the bond of peace."[56]

Does the Trinity Conjure Up Some Logical Questions for You?

For many people it does. Have you ever caught yourself wondering, "If Jesus *is* God, then . . ."

- Who died on the cross? Did God die? How can God die?

_____

- If He died and was God, who raised Jesus?

_____

---

[56]   Ephesians 4:3

- Why did Jesus proclaim that He did only what the Father told Him?

- If Jesus is God, how could He have been tempted by Satan?

- Why does Jesus constantly pray to God? Isn't He praying to Himself?

- Are His prayers real, does He really need something, or because He 'is God' are His prayers just for show?

- Why did He cry, "My God, My God, why have You forsaken Me?" Can He forsake Himself?

- How can Jesus be at God's right hand if He is God?

- Why did He say that no one knows the hour of His return, not even the Son? Does God hide information from Himself?

The trinity is a touchy topic because it is assumed that if you don't accept it that you doubt the deity of Christ or His existence before the world was founded. This simply is not true. The argument is presented as either/or with no room for revisiting the subject. The trinity as an explanation of God can be questioned without compromising any characteristic owned by Christ. Like many subjects that have such high political-like tensions, ears are often not willing to hear alternatives.

Does it have to be that way? Must we struggle so with a central tenet of our faith? Must we put up with the final argument that says, "Well, it doesn't make much sense, but we just can't expect to understand God?"[i] This is the haven people take when they are dogmatic about a doctrine they cannot explain. The doctrine of the trinity has put us all in a no-win situation. We are asked to believe what we cannot possibly understand. And has it also caused great misunderstanding?   If we cannot answer the questions above, we are missing precious truth about our Savior, truth that has been covered over. But maybe, just maybe, there is hope. Maybe it isn't the way we think it is.

The explanation of *non-scriptural* and *unscriptural* is repeated below from the chapter entitled "Did Creation Start with Poof"?

First, a non-scriptural phrase or word is, simply put, not part of the divine vocabulary. This doesn't mean that the thought thus represented is wrong but we should be on guard when using anything not found in Scripture as the danger exists that it leads us off track.

Second, is the concept or thought implied scriptural or *unscriptural*? This is where the 'rubber meets the road'. We need to be sure that the *idea* that these words represent is one that is supported by Scripture. Is it what Scripture means, no matter what words men have used to interpret it?

The non-scriptural test centers on *words* themselves and asks, "Do these words appear in Scripture?" The 'unscriptural' test centers on the *meaning* we attach to words. Are the meanings, or common understanding, of the words we are questioning found in Scripture?

What Do the Code Words Mean?

The words we use to describe the trinity are like secret codes: Godhead, God in three persons, the three are one, second person of the trinity, different persons but the same essence, fully God and fully man, God the Son, God the Holy Spirit, Jesus is God, and trinity. The key to decoding the mystery around these words is to unlock their meanings. We will look at just a few of these to help decode the trinity.

Unscriptural or Non-scriptural?

The first key is that they all share a common secret. They aren't in the Bible. Does that surprise you? We have heard them and used them so often that we don't realize that God does not use these expressions to describe Himself. Have we been numbed to accept words that are not God's? Are man's words acceptable? None appear in the pages of Scripture, yet we use them consistently to explain Who Christ is and His relation to God the Father.

We should not need to go beyond the vocabulary of Scripture to describe Who Jesus is. And certainly, we should not insist on using manmade words, phrases, and concepts to do so nor place the burden to believe in them on others. We will look at the code words that most often are used in explaining the trinity.

Trinity, the Word

Why not start with this word itself? What does it mean? It is a compound word from *tri*, meaning *three*, and *unit* or *unity* meaning *one*. Three-one. On the simple face of it, this is contradictory. This word is in conflict with itself. It is not sensible. Being the foundation of the concept, we should not be surprised if other expressions used to explain it are themselves contradictory. We are not disappointed.

The Three are One

The three are one: this is the meaning of trinity just stated more plainly. Now let's just think about this for a second. This asks us to believe that three equals one. As any child knows, 1 + 1 + 1 = 3. You may be thinking this is too simplistic and there are much deeper thoughts and truths surrounding this. What you need to do is strip away all the verbiage in your head and deal with these fundamentals, because they truly are the foundation of the concept. All the language we put on top of it can be no more clear or right than the foundation.

Three equals one is not an acceptable truth in mathematics. You would not accept this premise on which to start a business. We wouldn't go there in economics (3% is 1%), or work life (three paychecks are the same as one), or even to bake a cake (three cups are as good as one cup). Nor can we think of anywhere else that three different things are one same thing. This is what begins to put the mystical aura around the whole subject. And it also gives rise to the myriad analogies to explain this contradiction away. This idea flies in the face of what any rational person knows about three and one. Yes, it is that simple.

Are there three Gods or only one? We know the Scripture insists on one. Right away we have a conflict. The trinity concept insists that the Father, the Son, and the Holy Spirit are all God, which implies three Gods. So we must now make all three into one to preserve the one God of the Bible. That's a big mental gyration. And what is interesting is the length and verbiage people go to in order to explain it away. Error leads to error just like putting the wrong piece in a puzzle. Once you start that, you need the scissors. If you trim a little here and a little there, maybe they will all fit. You end up with a strange-looking picture and, inevitably, some pieces left over even the scissors can't fix.

> *The words contradict themselves*

Different Persons but the Same Essence

First, let's put this phrase down to its most simple form: different but the same. This is a fundamental and blatant contradiction. These words are opposites with opposite meanings. Because the phrase is in such basic conflict, people start expanding the vocabulary. In order to make three different things or beings into one same thing or being, words are added like 'persons' that share the same 'essence'. It sounds more educated and, to an extent, masks the fundamental contradiction. But it is just more puzzle trimming.

Once you start adding these words, you need to define them as well. What exactly is a person? I thought persons had bodies. Maybe not. What is an essence? Is there a difference between a person and an essence? When this doesn't satisfy, more verbiage is added. They are coequal in attributes yet subordinate in roles. None of these terms is well defined and only add murkiness to an explanation that grows more mystical by the minute.

There are three different persons but not three Gods. They are all 'fully' God and thus the same. That is supposed to mean (I think) that you don't have to add them together to get one good God out of it. But if you do add them together, you don't get more than one God.

Why all this extra vocabulary and large-sounding philosophical talk? It's a way of trimming the pieces until they fit. It's a way of obscuring the fundamental contradictions that, in other walks of life, we would dismiss as ridiculous. The added problem is that none of this vocabulary springs from God's words. We made it all up.

If we cannot explain God with His own words, we are on shaky ground. 'Three in one' has no basis in Scripture, and we find no 3-in-1 word like *trinity* (tri-unity).[57][ii] May I suggest that

---

[57]   1 John 5:7 If you read from the King James Version, you will read 'the three are one'. This is a well-known textual corruption by an

somewhere along the line, people thought that they must start with the trinity concept and prove that? So we have trimmed the pieces and created new words of explanation and put forth numerous analogies to make the picture look better, but it still distorts. May I further suggest we may want to throw this puzzle away and start over? Let's not start with a supposition that the trinity is true. Let's start with the supposition that the Scripture is true and see if it can lead to something we understand.

God the Son, God the Holy Spirit

Many explanations of the trinity begin by naming the three persons of the trinity as God the Father, God the Son, and God the Holy Spirit. A search of occurrences in the New King James yields this score:

God the Father—13
God the Son—0
God the Holy Spirit—0

God the Father wins by a landslide. The omission of the other two should be a huge clue. Sometimes what Scripture doesn't say is as loud as what it does say. Why do you suppose the latter two phrases are popular even though not found in Scripture? Could it be that these have crept into the vocabulary because we assume the trinity concept to be right and have supported it with non-scriptural terms? Their absence demands an answer. Maybe it just isn't the way we think it is.

Jesus Is God

One of the implications of the concept of the trinity is the insistence that Jesus is God. But what exactly is meant by Jesus *is* God? In the context of the trinity it doesn't quite mean that Jesus

---

overzealous group that wanted better biblical proof of the trinity. See note ii under this chapter in the end notes—it's pretty juicy!

is God the Father but still they are in some strange way the same. Roles and essences.

Let's start with the word god itself. If we are to discover whether Jesus is or isn't or in what way He might be God, we must know what the word means.

The word *god* is a title, much like the word *king*. The title God has the literal meaning of one who subjects persons to himself or put another way "one to whom others are subject." That is the definition of the word and why it can be applied to many other than the one true God.

Paul the apostle clarifies this:

> For even if so be that there are those being termed gods, whether in heaven or on earth, even as there are many gods and many lords, nevertheless for us there is one God, the Father, out of Whom all is, and we for Him, and one Lord, Jesus Christ, through Whom all is, and we through Him.
>
> 1 Corinthians 8:5–6 (CLV)

Our one God is the Father and our one Lord is Jesus Christ. Don't miss the point that Christ is the One through Whom all is. He is thus God's representative in all things.

The Hebrew word for god is elohim and is used for all gods, not just the one God of Israel. When Jacob was about to secretly leave Laban's household, Jacob's wife Rachel stole her father's images. Laban complains to Jacob:

> And now, go, yea, go, for you long longingly for the household of your father. Why have you stolen my elohim?"
>
> Genesis 31:30 (CLV)

The word 'god' is a title

I used the Concordant Version here especially to show that this word, elohim, is used for 'god' and for 'God' interchangeably just as it is in English. The word 'god' is a title and not a name.

Only the context can tell us which God, god, or gods are being referred to. When Moses inquired of God, "Whom shall I say sent me?" the answer was God's name, not His title. Tell them "I am" sent you. That is 'Yahweh', a name unique to our particular God. In fact the King James Version translates elohim with a capital 'G' meaning the God of Israel more than 2000 times, yet with a small 'g', god, more than 240 times and even 'goddess' twice[58]. Because it is a title (like manager or supervisor), the Scripture strives to make very clear which god and which lord it is talking about.

> For Yahweh your Elohim, He is the Elohim of elohim and the Lord of lords, the El, the great, the masterful and the fear-inspiring One, Who neither lifts up faces in partiality nor takes a bribe.
>
> Deuteronomy 10:17 (CLV)

Even if there are other gods, He is above them all. Even if there are other lords, He is the masterful One.

> For great [is] Yahweh, and praised greatly, And fearful He [is] above all elohim. For all elohim of the peoples [are] nought, And Yahweh the heavens has made.
>
> 1 Chronicles 16:25–26 (CLV)

As a title, the term 'god' could be used of anyone or thing to whom others might be subject. Even the lifeless idols were called 'gods' as people worshiped and sacrificed in subjection to them.

---

[58] The original languages in which the Scriptures were written do not use capital letters as we do. In fact, in the original, all letters are capitals so there is no way to distinguish between 'God' and 'god' other than the context. The choice of capital 'G' and small 'g' is an interpretation by English translators using the context as guide.

God Lends Out His Title
But what is a bit strange is that God Himself lends out His own title of God to others. Moses provides an interesting example when he resisted the job of being God's spokesman to Egypt.

> So the anger of the Lord was kindled against Moses, and He said: "Is not Aaron the Levite your brother? I know that he can speak well. And look, he is also coming out to meet you. When he sees you, he will be glad in his heart. Now you shall speak to him and put the words in his mouth. And I will be with your mouth and with his mouth, and I will teach you what you shall do. So he shall be your spokesman to the people. And he himself shall be as a mouth for you, and you shall be to *him as God*.
>
> Exodus 4:14–16 (NKJV); italics added

As God instructed Moses what to do and say, so Moses in turn instructed Aaron. Moses was 'God' to Aaron. He functioned as God's representative to Aaron. Of course, Moses wasn't God and wasn't close to being flawless, yet the Scripture says that he would be as God to Aaron because he would pass God's words to Aaron.

> Yahweh said to Moses: See, I appoint you as Elohim to Pharaoh; and Aaron, your brother, shall come to be your prophet.
>
> Exodus 7:1 (CLV)

Moses was God to Pharaoh, and by the time Moses left Egypt, I'll wager Pharaoh thought so too. And since Moses represented God, Aaron was Moses' prophet. Moses represented God, spoke the words of God, and performed the miracles of God. In those ways and instances he rightly wore the title of 'God'.

It is not so different in our human dealings. If Steve sends Gary to vote in his place (a proxy), the chairman will still call, "Steve, how do you vote?" Gary would shout, "I vote yes!" Since he is officially accepted in the place of Steve he can say I, meaning Steve, even though he isn't Steve. But he is rightly 'Steve' to that assembly.

The same thing happens at the national political conventions. "How does the great state of Tennessee vote?" "Tennessee votes yes!" Of course the delegate is not literally Tennessee, but he is authorized to represent it and therefore can be called 'Tennessee'.

It is extremely interesting that Jesus Himself addresses this issue of 'god' as a title.

> The Jews answered Him, saying, "For a good work we do not stone You, but for blasphemy, and because You, being a Man, make Yourself God." Jesus answered them, "Is it not written in your law, 'I said, "You are gods"'? If He called them gods, to whom the word of God came (and the Scripture cannot be broken), do you say of Him whom the Father sanctified and sent into the world, 'You are blaspheming,' because I said, 'I am the Son of God'?
>
> John 10:33–36 (NKJV)

God has called those to whom the word of God came 'gods'.[59] God did not consider it blasphemy to do so. We must remember that we capitalize to show respect and to distinguish the one true God. This is not true in either the Hebrew or Greek

Can Jesus be called God?

languages. This gives English readers a disadvantage especially in interpreting this case. In Greek Jesus would have said, "Is it not written in your law, 'I said, "You are Gods"'?" In other words, Jesus is saying that these men could rightfully have the title of God because the word of God came to them. Yet this did not make them the same being or essence as God. Therefore how much more would the Son of God wear and deserve the title of God (or Subjector)? Yet even

---

[59]   Psalm 82:6

in this instance He insisted only in the title Son of God. This point needs clear understanding. Jesus was only asserting Himself to be Son of God, yet the Jews react and say He made Himself out to be God. Jesus points out that God Himself gave the title 'God' to those men to whom the word of God came. Jesus is saying He claims a lesser title than God, but the Jews are still angry.

But to the Son [He] [says]:

> "Your throne, O God, [is] forever and ever;
> A scepter of righteousness [is] the scepter of Your Kingdom.
> You have loved righteousness and hated lawlessness;
> Therefore God, Your God, has anointed You
> With the oil of gladness more than Your companions."
>
> Hebrews 1:8–9 (NKJV)

This passage gives the title of God to the Son. Why? As King on the throne others are subject to Him. It is His rightful place. Yet, in turn, Christ has a God also, that is, one to whom He is subject. We can look through the lens of the trinity and be confused over the phrase, "Therefore God, Your God has anointed You." If Christ *is* God, how can He *have* a God? If they are the same, how can they be subject to themselves or each other? The trinity idea makes mishmash out of a simple hierarchy.

The God of Christ

The Head of Christ is God.

> 1 Corinthians 11:3 (CLV)

> Now when all things are made subject to Him, then the Son Himself will also be subject to Him who put all things under Him, that God may be all in all.
>
> 1 Corinthians 15:28 (NKJV)

One day, Christ Himself will relinquish His authority over creation granted by the Father and all will be directly subject to the Father, even Christ. Jesus Christ has One to Whom He is subject.

The implication of the phrase "Jesus is God" is that He must somehow be the same being as God the Father. But it is not at all necessary to press this point. We would not insist that Moses or Aaron is

Jesus has a God

the same as God the Father. Moses, Aaron, and the prophets all were called God. It is because they represented God in the words they delivered and miraculous acts they performed. Jesus represented God in words and deeds and a sinless life. The Son of God can be called God because He represents God the Father not because He is somehow the same as the one God. Yes, Jesus can be called God. And this, Jesus says, is not blasphemy.

Jesus Cannot Testify of Himself

Old Testament law states that no judgment of death can be taken without the testimony of two or three witnesses.[60] Certainly the person accused could not be one of the two or three even if he wanted to be. Even in our courts people are not expected to testify against themselves, and their testimony on behalf of themselves is not alone convincing. No, there must be third-party witnesses. Under this law Jesus was wrongfully put to death. No one stood as His accuser or testified to wrongdoing. Yet He had witnesses.

In the book of John, Jesus brings us three who testified on His behalf.[61] John was first, who announced Him with a baptism of repentance to prepare and make straight the road of the Lord.[62] But Jesus tells us that there is more than the testimony of mere man. He has two others: the works that He does and, most importantly, the Father Himself. It is significant to our subject

---

[60]   Deuteronomy 17:6
[61]   John 5:31-37
[62]   Matthew 3:3; Isaiah 40:3

that Jesus begins the revealing of these three witnesses with these words:

> If I bear witness of Myself, My witness is not true.
>
> John 5:31 (NKJV)

Jesus is asserting Old Testament law. You cannot testify on your own behalf. If Jesus is God, as the trinity would have it, then He bears witness of Himself in conflict with the law. If He is God but uses God as one of His witnesses, His testimony is not true. But His testimony is true as He brings us three others willing to testify, none of whom are Him.

The Trinity—A "Johnny-Come-Lately"

There is an interesting explanation in *The Anchor Bible Dictionary*[63] under the topic "Trinitarian Formulations":

> One does not find in the NT the trinitarian paradox of the coexistence of the Father, Son, and Spirit within a divine unity, the mystery of three in one, yet one does find there the data that serve as the foundation of this later dogmatic formulation.

The nice thing about folks who write dictionaries is that they tend to be the more objective people in our society. They are in charge of recording what is without judgment and without trying to make it what they would like it to be. When they work with words, they seek their current meaning—the way people actually use them—and past derivations—the way people used them in the past.

As this dictionary traces the trinity, they call it a "later formulation." In other words, it is a summary of what people

---

[63]   *The Anchor Bible Dictionary*, First Edition, Volume II, pg 1055, 1992. Doubleday.

think the data in the Scripture means. They also call it a dogmatic formulation. Try this one on from Webster's Dictionary: "Dogma—something held as an established opinion; a definite authoritative tenet; a point of view or tenet put forth as authoritative without adequate grounds."

The trinity fits the idea of a dogma. It is an opinion held so tightly that we are not supposed to question yet is without "adequate grounds." This "later formulation" came along several hundred years after the New Testament was written and compiled. Somehow those early Christians got saved, had a relationship with God, and knew His Son all without this dogmatic tenet. It is man's theory of how the pieces fit, code words that have come to be revered above the very words of Scripture.

What's Wrong with the Trinity?

The trinity is a confusion, a stumbling block to unbelievers who have no incentive to make sense of it. In a recent trip to Israel I discovered that it is especially an obstacle to Jews and Muslims, who see Christians as believing in three gods while they believe in only one. Even so, it has done far more damage within than without. It is a very loaded statement made all the worse by the pressure to accept it. There is a threat to believers that if they don't believe in the trinity they are not true believers. It is sometimes even insisted that if you question it you do not worship the same God. You must not be a Christian. What a dogmatic point this has been made over what is admittedly a doctrine even theologians struggle to understand. We should not be constrained to answer our beliefs in the context of the trinity. Scripture alone should suffice.

The trinity is man's attempt

The trinity seeks to represent God, but it misrepresents Him. It is often called the Holy Trinity as if it takes on a life of its own, as if we have created a new god. In a way, it is a false image. It does not properly represent God or His Son.

> And in vain they worship Me, Teaching [as] doctrines the commandments of men.
>
> Mark 7:7 (NKJV)

Part II
Who Do You Say I Am

Barely had the Jewish slaves been plucked out of cruel Egyptian hands by astounding acts of God when they returned to the gods of Egypt. There they were, fresh from the Red Sea at the foot of Mt. Sinai, waiting for Moses. But patience ran thin, and short of Moses' forty-day return, they made the golden calf, an altar for offerings, and worshiped the pagan gods of Egypt. Or did they?

Careful reading of these verses reveals a strange mix. They declare the calf to be the god that brought them out of Egypt. They had not forgotten entirely Who that God was. Aaron further establishes this by saying that "Tomorrow shall be a feast to Jehovah." That indeed is their God by name. Did the calf depict the gods of Egypt or did it represent Jehovah? There is reason to believe both.

> And he received [the] [gold] from their hand, and he fashioned it with an engraving tool, and made a molded calf. Then they said, "This [is] your god, O Israel, that brought you out of the land of Egypt!" So when Aaron saw [it], he built an altar before it. And Aaron made a proclamation and said, "Tomorrow [is] a feast to the Lord."
>
> Exodus 32:4–5 (NKJV)

The gods of Egypt afforded celebrations lustful and attractive. Under their license, the Jews gave the flesh free reign. Not so with the God of Israel.

Man makes images; God is not pleased

Even so, they could hardly deny the power that devastated Egypt on their behalf. The gods of Egypt would not likely destroy it to save its Jewish slaves. The golden calf was meant to represent Jehovah. This is the god "which brought you up out of the land of Egypt," they would declare. Intending to acknowledge Jehovah, we might reason that their heart was in the right place, yet we would join them in a great offense. God was not pleased in the slightest.

> And the Lord said to Moses, "I have seen this people, and indeed it [is] a stiff-necked people! Now therefore, let Me alone, that My wrath may burn hot against them and I may consume them. And I will make of you a great nation."
>
> Exodus 32:9–10 (NKJV)

What exactly made His anger burn so hot that He wished to completely destroy the entire nation and start over with Moses?

> And the Lord said to Moses, "Go, get down! For your people whom you brought out of the land of Egypt have corrupted [themselves]. They have turned aside quickly out of the way which I commanded them. They have made themselves a molded calf, and worshiped it and sacrificed to it, and said, 'This [is] your god, O Israel, that brought you out of the land of Egypt!'"
>
> Exodus 32:7–8 (NKJV)

Why the intense response? God is fiery mad. This is a place we need to pause and soak into. He is deeply offended. It was Him, Jehovah, they were depicting as an image of a dumb animal, a beast of His own creation, changing the glory of God into a four-footed animal.[64] We are as corrupt and corruptible as animals, yet we are insulted when we are compared to one. How much more the one Who has no corruption, the very Creator of the Universe?

---

[64] Romans 1:22-23

The Jews sought to bring Jehovah down to a manageable size. They wanted a god they could deal with, an image familiar to the gods of Egypt that would give them license.

Man Wants to See God

As the nation prepares to leave Moses to cross into the promised land, he warns again of this desire to carve a god for themselves.

> You must be very much on guard against your soulish desires (since you saw no physical representation at all on the day Yahweh spoke to you at Horeb from the midst of the fire) lest you should bring ruin on yourselves and make for yourselves a carving, a physical representation of any figure, a model of male or female.
>
> Deuteronomy 4:15–16 (CLV)

Remember at the foot of the mountain how God had talked to the whole nation directly? There was no form to see, no object to touch, just a thundering voice and the rumbling mountain filled with smoke and fire. They were plenty scared. So scared that they asked for Moses to step in. "We'll die if this continues." They couldn't take the heat. "You listen to God, Moses, and then tell us what He said." They weren't terribly afraid for Moses. He could go in the fire, he could be shrouded in cloud, and he could stand nose-to-nose with God on the quaking mountain. As for them, well, they would die!

Moses' last warning speaks of carvings as a 'soulish' desire, a fleshly desire. The flesh, above all, wants to save itself. They didn't want to die, and that's what it felt like to face the real God, the God of all creation. Their souls wanted a safer God, one that was more their own size. The flesh wants something different than a booming voice of pure truth. They wanted a God they could touch and see and control and, by the way, "we'll do the talking." The dumb animal figures don't talk, they don't make laws, they don't demand obedience, they don't expose sin, and they don't strike fear in our fleshly hearts.

While we wag our fingers at their stubbornness and their soulish desires, we do not often consider one of the motivations behind this and other idols that man has fashioned throughout the centuries: it is the deep desire to see God in three dimensions. To bolster our faith, we want to know what He looks like. Spirit though He may be, we want to see and hear and touch. The Greeks fashioned many gods, each to physically depict an aspect of the character of God. God is strong like Hercules, the author of love like Aphrodite, or like Neptune wielding the vast power of the sea. The point? The desire to see God may not in itself be wrong.

Man wants to see a god of his choosing

What is very wrong is to misrepresent God, the one true God, in any way that is not acceptable to Him. Each physical representation from a tree to a calf to Zeus degrades His holiness and debases His character and causes His anger to "wax hot against"[65] those that would make up God to suit their own eyes. Even in our culture with no intentional idol images, we have little understanding of the profound respect and honor due our Deity.

> Give to the Lord the glory [due] His name; Bring an offering, and come before Him. Oh, worship the Lord in the beauty of holiness!
>
> 1 Chronicles 16:29 (NKJV)

That calf, even of the most precious gold, could not in any way represent the "God Who brought you out of Egypt." And God would not have it. If we had any shred of an idea Who it is we are dealing with, we would shudder to talk with Him at all. So great is His holiness and intense His presence that we would die at the slightest crack of the throne room door. Isn't it a wonder how His anger is overcome by mercy and the wrath

---

[65]   Exodus 32:10

of His hand stayed by grace? Only the vast sufferings of Christ can demonstrate the chasm between our sinful impotence and a three times holy God Who holds power and dominion over every speck of this universe. To mold Him into the image of a calf, a lowly creature of His own making, is an offense of such enormity that it defies explanation.

> Now therefore let me alone, that my wrath may wax hot against them, and that I may consume them: and I will make of thee a great nation.
>
> Exodus 32:10 (KJV)

The Acceptable Image

Nevertheless He has answered that deep need to see Him physically. As much as God Himself has spoken fiercely against worshiping physical things and images, there is one image that is acceptable.

> Who rescues us out of the jurisdiction of Darkness, and transports us into the kingdom of the Son of His love, in Whom we are having deliverance, the pardon of sins, *Who is the Image of the invisible God*, Firstborn of every creature,
>
> Colossians 1:13–15 (CLV); italics added

Christ Jesus Himself, "the Son of His love," is the Image of God, acceptable in every way and in all ways. His thoughts, His actions, His attitudes, and even His physical form are and were complete and acceptable to represent His Father. God has provided an Image for us, physical, alive, and right.

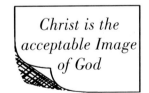

Christ is the acceptable Image of God

He has not ignored that innate human desire. When we take the fashioning of a physical god into our own hands, it ends very much as it starts, in corruption. Mankind's efforts tarnish God rather than exalt Him.

Is it any wonder that the Father declared at His baptism, "This is My beloved Son in Whom I am well pleased"?[66] And at His transfiguration, God the Father added, "hear Him."[67] Hear Him, see Him, put your hand in His side, Thomas. Know God by His Son.

It is no trivial matter that God's Son is His acceptable Image. The richness of its meaning unfolds as a bud reveals petal after petal, deeper and deeper beauty. Be expectant as familiar verses may take on new shape and hue.

> God no one has ever seen. The only-begotten God, Who is in the bosom of the Father, *He unfolds Him.*
>
> 1:18 (CLV); italics added

Yes, God the Father is invisible. God is spirit and has never been seen. It is the station of the Son to unfold Him, to explain Him, to let us see what He is like.

> God…has in these last days *spoken to us by [His] Son,* whom He has appointed heir of all things, *through whom* also He made the worlds; who being *the brightness of [His] glory* and the *express image of His person,*
>
> 1:2–(NKJV); italics added

The writer of Hebrews pounds home the point in language strong and bold. The word translated 'person' has in Greek the intent of a foundation or what underlies. 'Substance' is a better picture. The Son is the *express Image of His very substance.* Clear enough? But add now the *"brightness of His glory."* Honest questioners and detractors alike answer John 1:18 and his assertion that "no one has seen God" with a question, "Then who did Moses see?" Moses saw light. Moses saw the glory of God. Moses saw the Son, Who is the *brightness of*

His glory, Who represents Him perfectly in all ways and in every way. "God, no one has ever seen."

> "All was given up to Me by My Father. And no one is recognizing the Son except the Father; neither is anyone recognizing the Father except the Son and he to whom the Son should be intending to unveil Him.
>
> Matthew 11:27 (CLV)

How weak I seem when I shrink back in presenting the Son of God. People want many ways to God. People want options and tolerance of opinion. People want to create God in their image. People want many ways because they don't want to be confronted with sin. They want the permissive gods, the gods of the Egyptians. They want earn-your-way gods. They want to be acceptable in their own right.

How forceful and huge it is that there is only one way. "No one comes to the Father except through Me."[68] Of course! How could anyone come except through the very Image of the Invisible God? The very one through Whom all creation itself was made. The One Who has unfolded the Father to all creation.

When we see Christ we see God

Christ as the Image has unfolded God in numerous forms and perhaps thousands of ways.

> Moreover, brethren, I would not that ye should be ignorant, how that all our fathers were under the cloud, and all passed through the sea; And were all baptized unto Moses in the cloud and in the sea; And did all eat the same spiritual meat; And did all drink the same spiritual drink: for they drank of that spiritual Rock that followed them: and that Rock was Christ.
>
> 1 Corinthians 10:1–4 (KJV)

---

[68]   John 14:6

The Christ was the rock. He could have been the cloud that led them; He was the Word and the very Voice of creation.

Like the water of a large dam is channeled through the turbines for power, so the words of God were channeled through Christ to power creation itself. God accomplished creation through His Son. Christ must have spoken the very words, "Let there be light," yet behind Him was the power of the deity Himself.

Who is this Jesus, Peter?

> He said to them, "But who do you say that I am?" Simon Peter answered and said, "You are the Christ, the Son of the living God." Jesus answered and said to him, "Blessed are you, Simon Bar-Jonah, for flesh and blood has not revealed [this] to you, but My Father who is in heaven."
>
> Matthew 16:15–17(NKJV)

The Father of the Christ revealed it to Peter, "You are the Christ, the Son of the living God." This is not mere human knowledge, a piece of fisherman philosophy. Any other assertion or characterization as to His identity is not only unnecessary but is dangerous human tampering. Yet we cannot leave it alone. We must squeeze in that He is the second 'person' of the trinity. It is the beginning of image building and idol worship.

Who is this Christ? He is everything. God has invested in Him a trust so great it is difficult to imagine. God has pinned His entire plan for creation on the obedience of the Son to die for the salvation of the world and to fully represent the Father throughout time.

> Behold, a virgin shall be with child, and shall bring forth a son, and they shall call his name Emmanuel, which being interpreted is, God with us.
>
> Matthew 1:23 (KJV)

He who has *seen me* has seen the Father.

John 14:9b (CLV); italics added

When we see Jesus, we truly see God. Philip, the disciple, like many of us, did not understand this truth. It is a difficult thing to let sink in. If you have felt God to be distant and far from you, seek the Christ, the Son of the living God.

> Philip said to Him, "Lord, show us the Father, and it is sufficient for us." Jesus said to him, "Have I been with you so long, and yet you have not known Me, Philip? He who has seen Me has seen the Father; so how can you say, Show us the Father?
>
> John 14:8–9 (NKJV)

Philip knew that Jesus was not the same as the Father, but he didn't understand how Jesus completely represented the Father. The Pharisees called it blasphemy.

Emmanuel, God with us, the Son, the brightness of His glory, the Image of the invisible God, the Rock, the Cloud, the Word:

I want to know God. Know His Son.[69]

I want to see God. "Behold the Lamb of God."[70]

I want to hear You, God. "This is My Son, hear Him."[71]

---

[69] Luke 9:48b
[70] John 1:36
[71] Matthew 17:5

Part III
Discovering The Wonder of Christ

If the concept of the trinity covers rather than reveals, distorts rather than clarifies, then what have we missed? What don't we know about God and His Son that has been overshadowed by a "later dogmatic formulation"? Has the trinity cloaked from our eyes the very wonder of Christ? In this, more than anything else, we have been sadly shortchanged. Look at Christ afresh for what the Scripture says about His relationship to God.

An egg, three phases of water, a three-link chain, a triangle—all analogies that men have pursued to explain their version of God. Many who accept the idea of the trinity find fault with these in one way or another and sometimes offer their own. Why do we pursue these flawed notions when Scripture gives a clear and understandable analogy?

The great metaphor of Scripture
It is the metaphor of a Father and a Son. This is the cornerstone of truth concerning God and His Christ.

> "I shall be to Him for a Father
> And He shall be to Me for a Son"
>
> Hebrews 1:5b (CLV)

Christ and His God are not a literal father and son as we know it. They aren't human, and God, despite some who believe so, does not have a wife. But the metaphor well fits their relationship, and what's more, we well understand it. Rich with meaning and difficult to push too far, Scripture gives us the intimate picture of Father and Son. We don't need another one.

> The Father loves the Son, and has given all things into His hand.
>
> John 3:35 (NKJV)

How can we miss the tenderness and care that the Father has for the Son? So much is His love that God denied nothing to the Son. He receives the full inheritance of the Father. God's love is not without action. He trusts His Son and has given "all things into His hand."

We are proud of our children, especially at special moments like graduation. Each parent beams as their child makes his or her way across the stage and accepts the diploma. But in these ceremonies we can be somewhat frustrated. The larger the crowd, the less special our child becomes. There isn't often opportunity to single them out. Another smaller venue is needed if people are to listen to our praise for our child alone. When it happens, it is a unique moment. Perhaps at church or at a graduation party, the opportunity can be seized. And nothing seems to matter more than dad getting up and affirming the passage of his child into adulthood in front of a group of friends. "I am so pleased with who you have grown up to become."

What could make you feel better or more affirmed? Human sons and daughters sometimes wait years for a speck of encouragement or affirmation. Some never hear the longed-for words. But this, too, God the Father gives to His Son.

> And lo! a voice out of the heavens, saying, "This is My Son, the Beloved, in Whom I delight."
>
> Matthew 3:17 (CLV)

The Father was not ashamed of His Son, speaking words of love, comfort, and delight in front of His special people. It provides a compelling pattern for us. What child would not want to hear these words?

Father and Son, nothing explains their relationship better than this. Why do we turn from the great analogy of Scripture to a host of manmade notions that do not satisfy?

What, then, was and is the quality of this relationship? We learn much about the Son and His Father by answering this from Scripture. Try to go through these verses somewhat quickly so you build a total picture in your mind. The pertinent parts of each verse are in italic, especially since several verses are used more than once for illustrating different points.

Christ and His Father Are Different Beings

Begotten

For to which of the angels did He ever say:
"You are My Son,
Today I have begotten You"? And again:
"I will be to Him a Father,
And He shall be to Me a Son"?

Hebrews 1:5 (NKJV)[72]

Clear isn't it? Even the Old Testament speaks of how the Father begot the Son. And He is unique. Not even the angels can claim this position. But this is not all.

---

[72]   More support verses: John 1:14, 1:18; Acts 13:33

Firstborn

Who is the Image of the invisible God, *Firstborn of every creature.*

Colossians 1:15 (CLV)

Of all the creatures, Christ is first. This puts God's Son amongst the class of creatures.[iii] That is, He is a created being, which accords well with the idea that He is also 'begotten of God'. Where else would He come from?

For some reason people believe that if Christ was created that He is not all He should be or claimed to be. If God created Him to be His Son and granted Him authority, who are we to say that He is deficient? Was God's plan flawed? Believing that Christ was the first of all creation does not take away anything that Scripture asserts concerning Him.

Jesus Doesn't Act on His Own

Though he perfectly represents the Father, though He was with the Father from the beginning and the very instrument of creation, there are elements of authority and knowledge that are not His to give or to know. He does only what the Father desires.

He Speaks What the Father Speaks

seeing that I speak not from Myself, but the Father Who sends Me, He has given Me the precept, what I may be saying and what I should be speaking.

John 12:49 (CLV)

He Does What the Father Does

Jesus, then, answers and said to them, "Verily, verily, I am saying to you, The Son can not be doing anything of Himself if it is not what He should be observing the

Father doing, for whatever He may be doing, this the Son also is doing likewise.

John 5:19 (CLV)

There Are Things Only the Father Can Give and Know

He is saying to them, "My cup, indeed, you shall be drinking. Yet to be seated at My right and at My left is not Mine to give, but is for whom it has been made ready by My Father."

Matthew 20:23 (CLV)

But of that day and hour no one knows, not even the angels in heaven, nor the Son, but only the Father.

Mark 13:32 (NKJV)

The Father Is Greater

"You have heard Me say to you, 'I am going away and coming [back] to you.' If you loved Me, you would rejoice because I said, 'I am going to the Father,' for *My Father is greater than I.*

John 14:28 (NKJV); italics added

We don't have to mince these words. They are true as they sit. His Father really is greater than He. What a precious and glorious attitude. If anyone had the right to boast it was He. He is the favored Son, the apple of His Father's eye.

Meek am I and humble in heart.

Matthew 11:29 (CLV)

> Now Jesus said to him, "Why are you terming Me good?
> No one is good except One, God.
>
> Luke 18:19 (CLV)

Under our traditional viewpoint, we just don't believe this verse. Well, if Jesus 'is God', it can't be true; He has to be good. But that is not what this verse says. It says none is good except One, God. Jesus gives credit to His Father, the Source of good. If we are untangled from our confusion, we can believe what Jesus tells us.

Christ Has a Head

It is His Father to Whom He is subservient and from Whom His power and knowledge derive. He has a God.

> The Head of Christ is God.
>
> 1 Corinthians 11:3 (CLV)

Christ and His God

God the Father and Christ are not the same. Christ is the Image of the Invisible God.[73] One thing cannot be the image of another and at the same time be that thing. The golden calf was an image of a calf; it was not a calf. We would certainly not point to a live calf and declare, "There is a picture of a calf." If the Son of God is the Image of God, then He is not God. Yet He is God in two senses. First, we are subject to Him, and so He functions as a God (one who has subjects) to us though not as God the Father. Remember the word 'god' is a title and nothing more. Like being a company 'manager', many can hold the title. Second, if we have seen Christ, we have seen the Father. Since He is the perfect representation of God, when we have seen Him, we have seen God and the glory of God. It is not necessary to insist that any of this makes God the Father and His Son one being. Doing so

---

73   Colossians 1:15

goes beyond Scripture and, not surprisingly, conjures up more problems than it solves. These very problems have kept many unbelievers in unbelief.

Remember the Difficult Questions?

- Who died on the cross? Did God die? How can God die?
- If He died and *was* God, Who raised Jesus?
- Why did Jesus proclaim that He did only what the Father told Him?
- If Jesus is God, how could He have been tempted by Satan?
- Why does Jesus constantly pray to God? Isn't He praying to Himself?
- Are His prayers real, does He really need something, or because He is God are His prayers just for show?
- Why did He cry, "My God, My God, why have You forsaken Me?" Can He forsake Himself?
- How can Jesus be at God's right hand if He is God?
- Why did He say that no one knows the hour of His return, not even the Son? Does God hide information from Himself?

At every turn of a verse, the distinction between Father and Son permeates. God did not die on the cross. The Son of God died. One is Father and one is Son. A scriptural view easily answers our multitude of questions and untwists the entanglements of the trinity formulation.

God the Father and Christ are not the same

Nevertheless for us there is one God, the Father, out of Whom all is, and we for Him, and one Lord, Jesus Christ, through Whom all is, and we through Him. But not in all is there this knowledge.

1 Corinthians 8:6–7a (CLV)

"But not in all is there this knowledge." Isn't that an interesting place to put this phrase? You would think that this phrase would fit at just about any pronouncement of doctrine. Yet we find it here. It is directly pointed at our understanding of God and His Son and how easily it becomes twisted. There is one God *out* of Whom all is and one Lord *through* Whom all is. But not in the doctrine of the trinity is there this knowledge.

In All Ways Tempted as We

The cloud of the trinitarian idea obscures our view of the Jesus of earthy faith, gritty determination, and dogged obedience. This draw-in-the-dirt Jesus was more than we give Him credit for. Let's admit something that rolls around in the back of our minds we don't bring out often, if at all. We are told that He was without sin, and we are told that He was tempted by Satan. But haven't you ever thought in the deep recesses that we would expect no less from Him 'since He is God'? Don't we think He should be able to refrain from sin and resist the devil? After all, 'He is God'. What is so amazing about a sinless life or fulfilling the law when you are God? We don't like to bring these things up. They sound ungrateful and disparaging.

Yet these thoughts are there, and they rob us of a portion of belief. The logic says that this relationship between Father and Son, well, it isn't real. Not in the way we would experience it. Christ doesn't really need to pray to the Father. Maybe He just does it as an example for us. We tend in our heart of hearts to think He knows things He says He doesn't know. When it comes down to it, He doesn't need faith. But that is where the confusion and obscurity leaves us. We don't plumb the depths of His relationship or faith or hardship since somehow He, after all, is God.

If we meditate on the scriptural idea that He was and is a separate being, created the first of all creation to be the Son, His accomplishments can smack us with fresh and hard impact. I will challenge us that there are verses we don't really believe. Not thoroughly. Not down to the roots. We have skipped over them to avoid the inherent conflict between the picture portrayed by the trinity and the plain statements made by and about Jesus.

> For we do not have a High Priest who cannot sympathize with our weaknesses, but was *in all [points] tempted as [we] [are], [yet] without sin.*
>
> Hebrews 4:15 (NKJV); italics added

We can too easily nod in agreement with this verse. But that is not what we're feeling inside about His temptations. "No sir. No, He wasn't. You have no idea the temptations I have. How could He have been tempted by Satan's offer of power? It was easy for Him to answer, 'You shall not tempt the Lord your God.'"[74]

As I write, it is difficult for me to appreciate the truth of His temptation. Maybe my great temptation is to push back against this verse. Not openly of course. But down deep I want to go away in unbelief. How could the Son of God really be tempted by the sins I have indulged? He had some kind of protection I don't have. He had the angels, knowledge of His heavenly post, a better connection with the Father. Perhaps, but still it is a stark and plain statement: "in all points tempted as we." It is the second half of this truth that grates the nerves and opens wounds too raw and too harsh: "yet without sin."

Being tempted every bit as much as I: in greed, in falsehood, in lust, and arrogance and revenge and accusation. "Yet without sin." How, I wonder, could He have never entertained a lustful thought? Neither Solomon nor David nor Judah escaped its grip. I cannot face the ugly sinner that it makes me. If He was God, I am somewhat off the hook. The standard is inhumanly high. I can't be expected to…but if He was tempted exactly as I, my

---

[74]   Matthew 4:7

cover is gone. The animal skins are ripped back, and I am exposed in my nakedness and sin. There is no place to hide.

And then it dawns on me. Of course He had to be tempted as we. He had to face every ounce and every extreme of sin or there is no salvation. He was not here to polish the surface, to glide about on angel dust and skim the issues. There was no depth of corruption left behind, no dark sin that He did not touch.

There is an edge to the real Jesus. The mystical 3-in-1 Godhead Jesus, the we-can't-understand-Him Jesus is more easily dismissed. We can put our sins behind us and spend hours, days, even years, not understanding Him. It's misdirection, an avoidance of the gut problem. The real Jesus cuts to our soul. He lived as we live. He could have failed. He walked on the ridges of life, stood precariously on the pinnacle of the temple. He could have fallen. "Yet without sin."

Christ in the Garden

At the turning point of history, Christ feels a sorrow so deep and a burden so great that it defies us to grasp its meaning. We know that as He wrestled alone with the sin of the world, He literally sweat droplets of blood. The writer of Hebrews reminds us:

> Not as yet unto blood did you repulse, when contending against sin.
>
> Hebrews 12:4 (CLV)

We give in so easily to small everyday sins that we cannot fathom sweating in resistance to sin to the point of blood. His flesh, like ours, struggled to live, to have its way. He knew well He was to die and that on a cross. Had it not been prophesied many times and in many ways?[75] John would announce, "Behold the Lamb of God Who takes away the sin of the world."[76]

---

[75] Psalm 22
[76] John 1:29

How often He tried to tell his disciples of His impending sacrifice, but they could not understand. He rebuked Peter more than once for trying to stand in the way of His death. "Get thee behind me, Satan!"[77] What could have been surer or how could He have been more determined to become the sacrificial Lamb that He was sent to be? Yet listen afresh to His prayer in the garden.

> He went a little farther, and fell on the ground, and prayed that if it were possible, the hour might pass from Him.
>
> Mark 14:35 (NKJV)

How can He possibly pray that He might escape this hour? For this hour He was born. He knew "from the foundation of the world"[78] this plan of redemption in His blood. Did He not know that mankind hung in the balance? How marvelous and humble and astonishing is the answer.

> And He said, "Abba, Father, all things [are] possible for You. Take this cup away from Me; nevertheless, not what I will, but what You [will]."
>
> Mark 14:36 (NKJV)

With You all things are possible. In all of Scripture there may be no greater statement of faith. Despite the predictions, the prophecies of the Old Testament, and many of His own deeds already performed "in order to fulfill the Scripture," He prays and, yes, believes with You all things are possible. Does this mean He wants to forsake mankind? Does He wish to leave the world in sin? Far from it. He hopes that somehow God could accomplish redemption without this sacrifice. He doesn't know how. He can't even imagine how. He just believes that all things are possible with God. He puts practical knowledge behind and forgets all He knows of prophecy and prediction and plan

---

[77]   Matthew 16:22
[78]   I Peter 1:20

and rests totally and simply in the hand of His Father. Abba, Father, Daddy, You can protect Me and still redeem mankind. It is difficult to imagine both the depth and simplicity of this faith. Christ is not willing that any should perish. That hasn't changed. But the impending pain is so overwhelming that He asks that the impossible be made possible.

To the mind that bases all on experience and evidence, faith makes no sense. To call something that is not as if it were sounds insane. To grasp faith in the stern face of all law and logic is either supreme foolishness or confidence beyond description. In a sense it is a childlike faith, but how great is a faith that overcomes all adult sense and sensibility? The Son put Himself completely and fully in the hands of His Father—open, childlike and trusting. Had He not often told the disciples, "All things are possible with God"?[79] This was no idle statement for He would test it Himself. He would not forsake faith in God even in His darkest hour.

Yes, and if the Son believed it, God could have redeemed mankind at that late hour without the sacrifice of His Son. Do you believe that? All things are possible with God. Even so it was not to be. To somehow escape the sacrifice and see mankind redeemed was not the Father's will. Above all, He would do the Father's will. In this, too, is ultimate faith.

Not My Will but Thine

> And, being found in fashion as a human, He humbles Himself, becoming obedient unto death, even the death of the cross.
>
> Philippians 2:8 (CLV)

I have always wondered at the near sacrifice of Isaac. Abraham is featured as one with faith that God could raise the promised seed back to life. Parents shudder at the scene and marvel at

---

[79]   Mark 10:27

Abraham's resolve. There was Isaac, thrust upon the wood, his own father wielding the knife above his neck. Was Isaac a willing sacrifice? Did he share the faith of his father? "No matter what, God will take care of me." Was Isaac obedient unto death? Time and time again, verse after verse after verse, Jesus declares His utter dependence on the Father. He had to exercise faith that God would raise Him yet He was obedient unto death. While God risked His creation on trust in His Son, Jesus risked His life in faithful obedience. It was Abraham's faith, it was Isaac's faith, and it is our faith as well. We cannot extricate ourselves from the grip of death. If we foolishly suppose we can accomplish all other things under our own power, it is clear that this one thing is out of our control.

Yet this picture of Jesus' faith is muddied when we believe that He is God. This viewpoint changes His faith to mere process, a very painful experience to go through yet without the need for genuine faith. Was Jesus thrown around by the challenges of life, or because He 'was God', going through the motions but not the emotions?

But not what I will, but what Thou!

Mark 14:36 (clv)

There is a poignancy and a sharpness when we view verses like this against the backdrop that Jesus was and is a creature of God's making. He was and is His Son. How precious and important it is that Jesus looks up to God, does only what God shows Him to do, trusts His Father, and obeys. How real His temptations were and important His faith—we ride on its wings. He is a pattern for us who believe. If He fulfilled all that God the Father set before Him, then can we not trust Him? Indeed we cannot only rely on His finished work but can have greater appreciation for the remarkable obedience of the Son.

Keep It Simple and Scriptural

How are you to clearly explain your faith or in Whom you have believed? Can you do it from inside the tangles and snarls of the trinity? Over hundreds of years it hasn't gotten any better. It authors confusion, and God is not a God of confusion.[80] Why defend the indefensible and explain the inexplicable? Why not use the language and words of Scripture?

> *Thou art the Christ, Son of the living God*

Go for the heart of the matter. Talk instead of the wonders and courage, the faith and obedience, the humility and love of God's Son. Give the answer that Peter gave.

> He is saying to them, "Now you, who are you saying that I am?" Now answering, Simon Peter said, *"Thou art the Christ, the Son of the living God."* Now, answering, Jesus said to him, "Happy are you, Simon Bar-Jonah, for flesh and blood does not reveal it to you, but My Father Who is in the heavens.
>
> Matthew 16:15–17 (CLV); italics added

When they ask us Who this Jesus is we believe in, our answer is simple, "He is the Christ, the Son of the living God." Can there be a better answer? Happy are we, for flesh and blood does not reveal it to us, but our Father Who is in the heavens.

---

[80]   I Corinthians 14:33

Reflections

1. Have you ever been confused by the concept of the trinity? What is confusing?
2. Why do you think that the expressions, God the Son and God the Holy Spirit, aren't in the Bible?
3. The word 'god' is a title? How is this shown in the Scripture?
4. What attributes of Christ might we miss under the confusing statement that He 'is God'?
5. Please answer the question, "Who is Jesus?" using only the phrases of Scripture. Do you believe this is a sufficient answer without using the 3-in-1 proposition of the trinity?

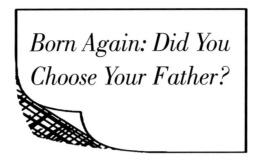

Born Again: Did You Choose Your Father?

Nicodemus has found his place in history as the guy who didn't get it. "Are you the teacher of Israel, and do not know these things?"[81] Jesus would say. We know the story of how Nicodemus made his way to Jesus by night. He was a teacher of Israel, a rabbi himself, not wanting to admit to the other Pharisees that he gave any credence to what Jesus said. Unlike the others, he did not come to weave a word trap for Jesus. Nicodemus genuinely wanted to understand.

> ### Common Belief
> If God is to be found, it is up to us to seek Him.

When Nicodemus tells Jesus that His signs demonstrate that He is truly from God, Jesus launches right into how Nicodemus can be included in the kingdom of God. No doubt there is much of the conversation we aren't privileged to read. Jesus uses the analogy of birth. He tells Nicodemus that he must be born again. Nicodemus wants to know how he could possibly re-enter his

---

[81] John 3:10

mother's womb, being a full-grown adult. Evidently he never went to the movies to see "Honey, I Shrunk the Kids."

We probably deem ourselves much smarter than Nicodemus because we get it. We get that Jesus speaks of being born again in the spiritual sense and that, in turn, means to be saved. Silly Nicodemus to stay in the fleshly realm. The rest of the passage just gives details of the analogy so Nicodemus understands it. We can safely proceed to John 3:16 since we get it.

Or do we?

Have we missed something by rushing past these verses? Have we understood so rightly what Nicodemus saw so wrongly? In some ways, I think Nicodemus has gotten a bad rap. This honest Pharisee has something to show us. Maybe, there's more here than we think there is.

Take a few moments to review the passage:

> There was a man of the Pharisees named Nicodemus, a ruler of the Jews. This man came to Jesus by night and said to Him, "Rabbi, we know that You are a teacher come from God; for no one can do these signs that You do unless God is with him." Jesus answered and said to him, "Most assuredly, I say to you, unless one is born again, he cannot see the kingdom of God." Nicodemus said to Him, "How can a man be born when he is old? Can he enter a second time into his mother's womb and be born?" Jesus answered, "Most assuredly, I say to you, unless one is born of water and the Spirit, he cannot enter the kingdom of God. That which is born of the flesh is flesh, and that which is born of the Spirit is spirit. Do not marvel that I said to you, 'You must be born again.' The wind blows where it wishes, and you hear the sound of it, but cannot tell where it comes from and where it goes. So is everyone who is born of the Spirit." Nicodemus answered and said to Him, "How can these things be?" Jesus answered and said to him, "Are you the teacher of Israel, and do not know these things?
>
> John 3:1–10 (NKJV)

First look at what Nicodemus did know instead of what he didn't. Nicodemus was not wrong about his physical interpretation. Let's give him credit for that. Yes, he took the whole example as physical, but in seeing his error, we tend to brush away the physical realities.

(In re-looking at the familiar phrase, *born again*, it might be best to jolt us out of our comfortable conception to adopt fresh wording. The Concordant Literal Version translates, "You must be begotten anew." We have said "born again" so often to mean "saved" that it is difficult to be objective about the root context of this expression.)

Nicodemus was so genuine in his desire to learn and believe that he pushed Jesus to explain how in the world he could fit back into his mother's womb. This question seems ridiculous, but Nicodemus wasn't a stupid man. He was a man on the road to true faith. (With God all things are possible).

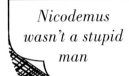

Nicodemus wasn't a stupid man

Let's take the story from there and follow what Jesus says:

> Jesus answered, "Most assuredly, I say to you, unless one is born of water and the Spirit, he cannot enter the kingdom of God. That which is born of the flesh is flesh, and that which is born of the Spirit is spirit.
>
> John 3:5–6 (NKJV)

When a baby is born it comes of water, the protective water of the womb. Born of water is all about the flesh. It's how we get here in the first place, but it does not make us fit to be in God's kingdom. We must be begotten anew, generated afresh, re-fabricated by the spirit. To be acceptable to God we must be born of the spirit. Flesh and blood, we are told, cannot inherit the kingdom of God.[82]

---

[82]   I Corinthians 15:50

Along with Nicodemus, we now know there are two births available. But Jesus gives us more than we bargained for. Now we come to a statement we probably have not well considered.

> You should not be marveling that I said to you, 'You must be begotten anew.' The blast is blowing where it wills, and the sound of it you are hearing, but you are not aware whence it is coming and where it is going. Thus is everyone who is begotten by the water and the spirit."
>
> John 3:7–8 (CLV)

Mysterious thing this blast, this wind; it blows where it wills, not where we will. We can't go get it, and we can't send it on its way. How forceful and fearful it can be. It moves seamlessly and invisibly, bringing warmth, welcome moisture, or unspeakable destruction. We know it only by its effect on objects: the sway of the tree, the whistle in the canyon, the pressure against our faces. It is otherwise invisible. If only we could corral the wind. We can try to grab it, but it slips through our fingers until our fists are clenched around nothing at all. Where does it come from, this invisible force? Where is it going?

It is fickle in its twists and turns. One moment it comes from the west, and a few moments later the northeast. It is called by many names: tornado, breeze, hurricane, current, storm. We know one thing: friendly and fierce, the wind is not under our control. Even our sophisticated weather satellites and computer models cannot plumb its mystery. "We are getting a storm from the northwest," they tell us. Yes, it would seem we have discovered where the wind comes from. But where did the northwest get it? Searching for the source of the wind is like trying to find the beginning of a carousel. Predictions of where it is going often find the weatherman red-faced. "The storm completely missed us!" Despite our technology, we really don't know where it is going.

But Jesus is not talking about the literal wind. He is talking about the spirit and how it is like the wind. The Scriptures often use the wind to explain the character of spirit.

When God filled his nostrils with air, life began for Adam.

> And the LORD God formed man [of] the dust of the ground, and breathed into his nostrils the breath of life; and man became a living soul.
>
> Genesis 2:7 (KJV)

This action of the spirit goes beyond Adam. In the book of Job, Elihu asserts ,

> The Spirit of God hath made me, and the breath of the Almighty hath given me life.
>
> Job 33:4 (KJV)

Job 34:14 tells us that if God were to withdraw His spirit, all flesh would perish. Not just believers, but all would perish. God keeps all alive by supplying the breath of life. The song is right when it asserts, "You are the air I breathe," for indeed He is.

The Greek word for spirit is *pneuma* from which we get our word pneumatics, things having to do with air. It literally means blow-effect or the effect of blowing. Wind is the physical representation of spirit. When you do something as simple as blowing on your hand, you know you have God's spirit, the breath of life, energizing you and keeping you alive. Though this is not the same as the Holy Spirit making its home in you,[83] it does demonstrate God's active work in His world. The earth of which Adam was formed took no life until God breathed into it the spirit of life.

> Thus says the El, Yahweh Elohim, Creator of the heavens, Who stretched them out, Who stamped the earth and its

---

[83]   I Corinthians 3:16

offspring, Who gives breath to the people upon it, and spirit to those going in it.

Isaiah 42:5 (CLV)

This word *pneuma*, spirit, is the same word used for *wind* or *blast* in John 3:8;

The blast [spirit] is blowing where it wills, and the sound of it you are hearing, but you are not aware whence it is coming and where it is going. Thus is everyone who is begotten by the water and the spirit."

John 3:8 (CLV)

Jesus invites us to understand that the spirit blows where it wills. The powerful word in this verse is 'thus'.

Thus is the spirit. Fierce and friendly, the "power of the Most High"[84] goes where it wills and only its sound can we hear. We know only its effect. It strikes a heart and a new birth begets newness of life. Suddenly one more soul is fit for God's kingdom. We can't summon the spirit. We can ask, we can plead, but we can't call in the breeze to do its work. We must wait on the spirit as we wait upon the wind. We cannot bring it on ourselves nor can we send it to another. It happens when it happens and it travels where it wills.

The spirit blows where it wills

Just as you do not know what the way of the wind may be, Or how bones are formed in the full womb. Thus you cannot know the work of the One, Elohim, Who made everything.

Ecclesiastes 11:5 (CLV)

The spirit acts on everyone thus whether in their first birth or their second. It makes a lot of sense if we consider our physical

---

[84]   Luke 1:35

birth. How much warning did we have regarding our first birth? What kind of work did we put in to make sure we were born? Did we help God? Were we in control? Did we select our parents? In fact, we have such lack of control even as parents that we still rightly call it "the miracle of birth." Just as we did not self-determine nor anticipate our first birth, 'thus' it is with our second birth. We are God's choice in the matter of both. The wind (spirit) blows where it wills, not where we will. Isn't it also obvious that we need first to arrive in the physical birth of the water of the womb or we cannot be born of the spirit? The fact that there is a likeness, an analogy, between the fleshly birth and spiritual birth does not take away the literal meaning of either. They are both quite literal and very necessary!

Spiritual birth is, if anything, a greater miracle than physical birth. We are reminded how Paul tells Timothy, "The Lord knows who are His."[85]

> Jesus answered, "Most assuredly, I say to you, unless one is born of water and the Spirit, he cannot enter the kingdom of God. That which is born of the flesh is flesh, and that which is born of the Spirit is spirit.
>
> John 3:5–6 (NKJV)

Nicodemus didn't understand being born of spirit. At his time and in his place we would likely have been as blind to the spirit as he. But like Nicodemus we can use what we know of physical birth to recognize the character and need of spiritual birth. And what we should know is that we must have the second birth, and we are helpless to make it happen.z

---

[85]   II Timothy 2:19

Can We Take Credit for the Spirit's Arrival?

At times we catch ourselves being smug in our salvation. Next to unbelievers going in wrong directions, as they often do, and being, as Paul says, "without God in the world,"[86] we see they haven't chosen God. We can tend to feel a bit proud that we at least have made the right choice. In fact, we have made the righteous choice. Intellectually, we would claim it is all grace and all God. Yet in some deep place where our emotions and thoughts merge, we want to be right compared to others being wrong. We seek a smidgeon of self-justification, our own righteousness in believing, instead of God's righteousness in justifying.

When we take internal inventory and sense those feelings welling up inside, we would do well to remember the wind. Had the spirit not chosen to come upon us, we could neither perceive nor enter the kingdom of God. Many of the Jews were blinded to the kingdom and rejected the King. The wind drove around them; they could not perceive the kingdom. The difference between the believer and the unbeliever is the will of the wind. "Where then," the apostle would ask, "is boasting? It is excluded."[87] If we arrived on the planet by our own willpower we might be justified in boasting. We are as justified to boast in our physical birth as we are in our spiritual—which is to say we are not justified in either.

Beyond being humble and thankful for both births, what is the point? Well, that is the point. For if the spirit's choice is of God and not of us, then we owe Him profound thanks and praise. Our humility should be in direct proportion to His Power. He alone can save a soul, make a new creation, cause a second birth. This is no wayward wind to God for He alone directs where the spirit blows. For us, we feel profoundly fortunate to have been in its path.

---

86   Ephesians 2:12
87   Romans 3:27

For by grace you have been saved through faith, and that not of yourselves; [it] [is] the gift of God, not of works, lest anyone should boast. For we are His workmanship, created in Christ Jesus for good works, which God prepared beforehand that we should walk in them.

Ephesians 2:8 (NKJV)

Reflections

1. What unique analogy does the Scripture use for the spirit?
2. How does the Nicodemus story show that God chose you and you did not choose Him?
3. Does it feel like you chose God? If so, how can you resolve this with Scripture?
4. Do you sometimes feel as if you chose to believe God? Is there a difference between your feelings and your thoughts? If so, how do you resolve this?
5. Is your gratitude likely to be greater if God chose you or if you chose Him? Why?

The Homosexual: Made or Born?

I arrived in San Diego seven hours after a distress call I had received from my cousin who, you need to know, is a homosexual. His mental state was so fragile that I realized I had to catch the next available flight, hoping that he wouldn't do anything rash before I arrived. He had moved away from Denver, his family, and his support system to open a restaurant in San Diego and, as it actually turned out, to abandon any connection with biblical restraints. We never rejected him, but our presence was a constant reminder of God's injunction. He wanted to be able to go whole hog and chase the desires of his flesh to the fullest.

> **Common Belief**
>
> *God would not allow a person to be born with a homosexual preference.*

When I found him at his restaurant, he was on the verge of a nervous breakdown. His restaurant was broke; he had attempted suicide by throwing himself in front of a moving car on a busy San Diego boulevard and was incapable of making any decisions. In twenty-four hours I helped him (and pushed him) to close

down his business, negotiate out of his remaining lease, terminate
the few employees left, leave his male roommate, and fly back to
Denver. It took several months for him to regain stability. For
almost one year, he carried his Bible under his arm everywhere
he went like a landlubber might clutch a life preserver. It was his
only link to life. He returned from that experience HIV positive
and has been fighting AIDS ever since. I saw firsthand how this
so-called 'life style' deals out death.

The experience with my cousin begged the question of why
people become homosexual in the first place. Do you believe that
the desire for the same sex is a choice or do you think people are
born that way? Or do you think it even matters?

I'll tell you what I have heard. I have heard many Christians
say that homosexual desire is a choice. It is a sin, and the
homosexual chooses to sin. If they choose to sin by being with
the same sex, they can also choose to stop sinning and direct their
desires toward the opposite sex. Besides, these people go on, God
wouldn't make someone sin. He wouldn't create them that way
from birth. God doesn't make junk.

(Before we go too far, you should know that I am assuming
homosexual behavior, male or female, is a sin, contrary to God's
design, contrary to His law, and indecent in His eyes. I have no
intent to substantiate this. If you are unsure on that point, I will
leave you with two Scriptures and go on about our business.[88]
Also, I will use the male pronoun for convenience but to be
inclusive of both sexes.)

What makes this line of thought even more compelling is the
opposite view. If the homosexual desire is inbred, if it is part of
the body's makeup at birth, then it implies the behavior cannot be
helped. What can homosexuals possibly do about it? They were
born that way. And if they really can't help it, then the Christian
view that the behavior is a sin becomes difficult to enforce. We

---

[88]   Romans 1:26; Leviticus 20:13

don't feel like we can ask them to quit when it really isn't their fault. It puts us between a rock and a hard place. We don't want to succumb to the world's view that right and wrong depend on the situation. We rightly revolt at the promotion of homosexuality as a lifestyle. The culture around us pushes acceptance as the highest virtue as it redefines this destructive and unnatural practice. We must stand against a depraved culture and draw the clear line of sin that Scripture draws around homosexual activity. We don't like the idea that people are born that way because it gives excuse to the sin and weakens our ability to uphold God's clear mandate.

How we react to homosexuality depends on our opinion of why it is here. If homosexuality is a choice, then we tend to feel justified in shunning the homosexual and looking in disgust at his sin. People who have a normal desire for the opposite sex have a difficult time empathizing. It is easy to be disgusted. This becomes the reaction at many churches. They shun the homosexual, having no interest in restoration. They feel compelled to take action against sin, and indeed they shouldn't just let it slide.

On the other side, if we believe they are born that way, then sympathy for their condition is easier to come by. We tend to extend love more easily. We are less likely to shun them and more likely to accept them. But this approach also easily leads to becoming numb to the sin. We prefer extending love to drawing a clear line. Without intending to, we end up acting out the worldview that says this behavior is a lifestyle. With this approach, we can avoid the confrontation, justifying inaction by saying "We have no right to point out someone else's sin."

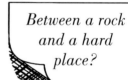

Between a rock and a hard place?

No matter which side you choose, born or made, we are called upon to love one another. Are we between a rock and a hard place? I hope we aren't. I hope it isn't the way we think it is.

Do I believe you can be born with a desire for the same sex? Yes I do. But I don't need the story of my cousin to convince me. Neither do you. I hope you are holding out for light from God's Word to corroborate experience.

Let's go back to the basics. Somewhere in the garden sin happened, and through sin the death process began. No one has been born since who is not already dying and who doesn't have sin operating in his mortal body.

> Therefore, even as through one man sin entered into the world, and through sin death, and thus death passed through into all mankind, on which all sinned
>
> Romans 5:12 (CLV)

Sin reigns in death says the Scripture.[89] This is not confined to the sins we do but includes the principle of Sin we are born with from the start. Is this true from our experience? Of course. We see it every day. People are born with every conceivable malady. They are born missing limbs, with Down syndrome, missing part of the brain, hooked to one another, with defective or missing organs. That is the death principle at work in us because of original sin (not the sins we commit). We live in a broken, fallen, distorted world. We live in a world that isn't right. But, you say, none of those defects would cause someone to sin. Really? What about the alcoholic who has a compelling affinity from the very first drink he takes? How does that happen? People are born with two sets of sexual organs. What are they and what is sin to them? What do you do with that? "God doesn't make junk" doesn't seem to cover that problem very well.

We should not expect rightness to come out of a world that is in wrongness. People can be born with a desire for the same sex just as sure as people are born with every other imaginable problem. It isn't difficult to discern those born with this defect.

---

[89]   Romans 5:21

Most of us can tell a homosexual male in about five seconds. They have a characteristic way of talking and walking. Comedians make a living imitating them. That is not a choice; it is an effeminate chromosome hiding in there somewhere just as surely as Down syndrome has physical characteristics.

So now what? Are they exempt from the law? If they can't help it, are they off the hook?

> Now if what I am not willing, this I am doing, I am conceding that the law is ideal. Yet now it is no longer I who am effecting it, but Sin making its home in me. For I am aware that good is not making its home in me (that is, in my flesh), for to will is lying beside me, yet to be effecting the ideal is not.
>
> Romans 7:16–18 (CLV)

What we read is that we are all under sin; no one escapes it. Sin makes its home in us. We aren't perfect. We are born physically imperfect and that means that we not only die but we also do things we rather wouldn't. We struggle constantly with our sin and our sinful bodies. We can scarcely stay on a diet for more than a week. Some people were born with a high propensity toward chocolate. Just can't stay away from it. Our bodies (that is our flesh) are born with certain cravings always tugging at us.

Some crave donuts and some alcohol, some gambling and some pornography. Most men have a desire to see the female form. It causes them to sin. They didn't invent that desire themselves; they were born with it. Is that a good excuse to be involved in pornography? A very few have been so fiercely gripped by pornography that they take it and it takes them to the extreme of serial murder. We label them sick, but they are just exhibiting the extremes of sin. Who can avoid it?

> But the Scripture locks up all together under sin, that the promise out of Jesus Christ's faith may be given to those who are believing.
>
> Galatians 3:22 (CLV)

It says we are locked up under sin. We can't escape on our own. If we understand the basics of sin, we shouldn't be surprised that some are born homosexuals. If that is true, then how can we blame them or anyone for the sins they do? Is it fair to ask them to stop?

> Let not Sin, then, be reigning in your mortal body, for you to be obeying its lusts.
>
> Romans 6:12 (CLV)

In other words, don't do it. Scripture doesn't let anyone off the hook. Not the alcoholic, not the greedy, not the homosexual, and not the serial  murderer. It is simply incorrect to believe that if someone is born that way that they are absolved of accountability. According to God, in one way or another, we are all born that way.

We are locked up under sin

Does this mean if homosexuals are born, then they aren't made? Not at all. One does not exclude the other. If we keep in mind the basics of being under sin, then it is very clear that someone could take the reins off their lust until they don't care where they get satisfaction. A normal heterosexual could have such a desire for sex that he eventually takes it to the same sex. Sin is still the central problem, and they, too, are not off the hook. On the surface we might trace some sins to volition and some to inherent problems in the body. At the very root sin is always a birth problem. That's how we come from the factory.

That puts us in one heck of a mess. We are trapped by sin and commanded to avoid it. What shall rescue us? The Apostle Paul wasn't much happier with this setup than you or I.

> A wretched man am I! What will rescue me out of this body of death? Grace! I thank God, through Jesus Christ, our Lord. Consequently, then, I myself, with the mind, indeed, am slaving for God's law, yet with the flesh for Sin's law.
>
> Romans 7:24–25 (CLV)

His answer is clear and positive. It is God's grace that will save us. It is the power of faith in Christ that allows us to overcome sin. With the commands to avoid sin, God has given us the tools to do so. We don't have to muster up the willpower, for this is a free gift.

God's Law Is Good

> Now if what I am not willing, this I am doing, I am conceding that the law is ideal.
>
> Romans 7:16 (CLV)

What is so ideal about this law that points out our sin? We can see why it is so good by considering the consequences of disobeying God's laws. The more we clutch to money and possessions, the less happiness we buy. The more we lie, the less we are told the truth. The more we eat, the less energy we have. The less we forgive, the less peace we have. Homosexual behavior is against God's law, and the homosexual, by and large, leads a lonely, unstable, unsatisfied, and statistically, a shorter life.

We can empathize with the homosexual as his plight is everyone's plight. It is the plight of sin. But we need not compromise on denouncing his sin and calling it what it is. We do him no favors in glossing over his self-destruction in the name of love. In the name of love we should face him with it. It is not love to passively look on while people pursue a 'death style'.

Don't make the mistake of believing that recovery for the homosexual is always going to end up in desire for the opposite sex. It may not work that way. For some recovered alcoholics, casual drinking is not in the cards; his new freedom is based on abstinence for life. The homosexual from birth doesn't need the extra pressure of being something he is not, of others measuring his repentance or holiness or sincerity based on flipping the switch of his sexual preference. Perhaps God will change his desires, and that is a blessing. Otherwise he will need all the help he can get to pursue a new life of abstinence, of celibacy.

How Should We React to Sexual Sin?

Sexual offenses are dangerous, not only to those involved, but to those in their close circle or, in this case, in the same family of faith.

> But now I have written to you not to keep company with anyone named a brother, who is sexually immoral, or covetous, or an idolater, or a reviler, or a drunkard, or an extortioner—not even to eat with such a person.
>
> 1 Corinthians 5:11 (NKJV)

We are to separate from those involved in intense sin. This is for their restoration and not for eternal banishment. There is a story in First Corinthians of a man discovered having sex with his father's wife. The passage puts this sin under the general category of prostitution and instructs the believers,

> To give up such a one to Satan for the extermination of the flesh, that the spirit may be saved in the day of the Lord Jesus.
>
> 1 Corinthians 5:5 (CLV)

It sounds like an ugly process, to exterminate the flesh, but the flesh is at war with the spirit, and above all else the spirit must be saved, for both the one committing the sin and others of the group whose flesh is tempted to follow a similar path. Our goal is to help each other be holy and blameless,[90] so we are to . . .

> Clean out, then, the old leaven, that you may be a fresh kneading, according as you are unleavened.
>
> 1 Corinthians 5:7a (CLV)

> Expel the wicked one from among yourselves.
>
> 1 Corinthians 5:13b (CLV)

Our current Christian culture views this prescription as too harsh and actually ineffective, making it easier to avoid the confrontation. We have fallen away from God's methods, thinking ourselves wiser than He, adopting either acceptance, based on loving everybody, or more rarely these days, permanent expulsion. God presses the more difficult remedy of confrontation and separation, ultimately seeking restoration through heartfelt repentance. Through this process, the man in our story is brought to repentance.

> This punishment which [was] [inflicted] by the majority [is] sufficient for such a man, so that, on the contrary, you [ought] rather to forgive and comfort [him], lest perhaps such a one be swallowed up with too much sorrow. Therefore I urge you to reaffirm [your] love to him.
>
> 2 Corinthians 2:6–8 (NKJV)

I am convinced my cousin was born with homosexual desire. Somewhere in the middle of high school, he began to notice that he was different from the other guys. It isn't something he made up or wanted for himself. He grew up around two brothers and me in the early years. None of the rest of us experiences this tendency. Like an alcoholic, he is now recovering. But like an

---

[90]   Ephesians 1:4

alcoholic, you don't really recover. True alcoholics can't ever take a drink. They have a propensity toward alcohol. It does something in their bodies that it doesn't do in other people. My cousin would love to be normal. He would do most anything to have the desire for a woman, get married, settle down, and have a family. But he can't. He just isn't wired that way. He has come to understand homosexual behavior to be a sin. He has given up the lifestyle and its destructive patterns. In fact, the destructive results got his attention and not God's proclamation against it.

He would have long since changed if he could have. He is between a rock and a sin place. By stopping his homosexual behavior, he gives up a lot. Think about it. If he has no desire for a woman and can't give in to the desire for men, he must choose a celibate life. He is essentially alone. He is not without desire, just without a partner.

Still, it was a wonderful feeling to see him rescued from the tangles of the flesh and rediscover hope in his Savior. We must know that it is often accomplished through tough love. Many parents have been criticized by Christian friends for rejecting their son or daughter for homosexual behavior. When parents, realizing the devastation of this behavior,[91] are looking for repentance and restoration, they should be commended and supported for doing it God's way.

In the end, it doesn't matter whether the homosexual is born with that tendency or it is the next step in a downward spiral to satisfy the flesh. Either way it must be called out as sin, cleansed from the church, and the person provided a loving pathway back when repentance has done its work. Will they always return? Will it always work? Sadly, no. As sinners we often choose the pathway of the flesh rather than reliance on God. But that is no reason to drift from God's way of restoring a Christian brother or sister.

---

[91]   Romans 1:27

God's rules are ideal because they are the ideal way for us to live. He came to give us life and that more abundantly.[92] It is for our good. Father knows best. We aren't between a rock and a sin place. We are between Christ our Rock and a Grace place.

> *We are between Christ, our Rock, and a Grace place*

Reflections

1. What have you believed in the past concerning homosexual desire? Was it by choice, a born trait, or both?
2. What fundamentals about sin can answer the above question?
3. What is the biblical solution to intense sin in the family of God?
4. Are there people in your life for whom you need to adjust your approach to help them toward repentance?
5. What if you follow God's approach and the one you care for is not restored? What if you are criticized because it doesn't work? Does it make God wrong?

---

[92]   John 10:10

Did Creation Start with Poof?

What is creation? I mean down at its roots, down where God called light into being, down where the beginning began. We lay claim to being creative, yet in the shadow of God working in those primordial moments when light and earth, sun and moon, animal and man found their place, is it a frivolous claim? We humans make things but always from other things. Is there a difference between how men create and how God creates? What is true creation? Take a few moments to describe your own notion of creation. (If this is not your book, get permission or get a pencil!)

Common Belief
God creates something out of nothing.

_____

_____

_____

_____

Are there Scriptures that come to mind that would back up your definition?

_____

_____

How did you do? Many say something like, "The true miracle is that God creates something out of nothing whereas man must take current substances and change them." The popular notion is that God starts with nothing and poof! Things appear.

Ex nihilo, a Latin phrase meaning "out of nothing," is often used to describe this viewpoint of God's amazing creation. Humanly, we do not create the substance or stuff of things. What amazes us is a God Who has created the stuff of which all else is formed. At first blush it would seem as if crediting God for creating something out of nothing functions to show His greatness against man's inability. It's a trick we haven't been able to duplicate. And so, we are satisfied that God is glorified in this explanation.

We could leave it right there, right where it has been for centuries. Yet things aren't always as they seem. The first answer, often being the most obvious answer, isn't always the right answer. We need to dig deeper. What has God Himself said? Only His Own words can tell us if "of nothing" is the right label to put on His work of creation. Does it give Him the glory He deserves?

The tests we will use both center on God's inspired word. Just as Paul admonishes Timothy to use a pattern of sound words,[93] we always want to scrutinize our words when we summarize any concept we believe comes from Scripture. So first we ask, are these words themselves found in Scripture or are they instead non-scriptural? A non-scriptural phrase or word is, simply put, not part of the divine vocabulary. This doesn't mean that the thought

---

[93]   II Timothy 1:13

conveyed is wrong, but we should be on guard when using words not found in Scripture as they could lead us into error.

Second, is the concept scriptural or unscriptural? This is where the rubber meets the road. We need to be sure that the idea that these words represent is one that is supported by Scripture. Is it what Scripture means?

Non-scriptural?

We find by applying our first test that the Latin phrase *ex nihilo*, "out of nothing," is not found in Scripture. Since the original Scriptures were not written in Latin, this phrase, if we could find it, would have been a translation of either Hebrew or Greek. But it is not found in those original languages of Scripture either. "Out of nothing" is not found anywhere and especially not near the contexts discussing creation or formation. So, we classify the phrase ex nihilo as non-scriptural since it is not found in the text. In itself this discovery would not condemn its use, yet it should automatically raise the next question.

Is it Unscriptural?

If this phrase does not appear in creation contexts, what phrases show up and what do they say? Here are a few:

> For even if so be that there are those being termed gods, whether in heaven or on earth, even as there are many gods and many lords, nevertheless for us there is one God, the Father, *out of Whom all is*, and we for Him, and one Lord, Jesus Christ, through Whom all is, and we through Him. But not in all is there this knowledge.
>
> 1 Corinthians 8:5–7 (CLV); italics added

Concerning creation, the Bible tells us that there is one God "out of Whom all is." Is this phrase equivalent to "out of nothing" or does it have a different meaning? For the phrases to be literally equal, we would have to conclude that God has the same meaning as nothing. As they say in the south, "That doesn't set too well." The one God Who created everything didn't create it 'out of nothing' but 'out of Himself'."

> For even as the woman is out of the man, thus the man also is through the woman, yet *all is of God*.
>
> 1 Corinthians 11:12 (CLV); italics added

These Scriptures assert "all is of God." In fact, more literally in the Greek, "all is *out* of God." Isn't this quite a contrast to the notion that "all is made out of nothing"? Is this difference important? After all, we meant that God was the source when we said He created things out of nothing (ex nihilo). Really? Is this, as they say, just semantics or do words have meaning and force?

All is of God

These two phrases represent two vastly different ideas. God is not "nothing." He is "something." What is that something that all else comes from? Knowing that God is spirit,[94] we have a difficult time picturing that the phrase "all is out of God" could be quite literal. I suggest that it is vitally important that the very substance of things is not out of nothing but out of God Himself. He is not a magician pulling rabbits out of a hat, making things appear out of thin air. He makes things from Himself. It may be difficult to imagine how this might be. What could it mean, "all is out of God"? By rights we should be content to believe the Scripture and leave it at that. Lucky for us that science unlocks some of God's mysteries, allowing us to grasp a little easier how these things might be.

Albert Einstein theorized a relation between energy and matter. His simple equation had profound implications:

---

[94]   John 4:24

$E = MC^2$

Energy = Mass times the Speed of Light^2

I don't pretend to understand why this relationship exists or to enter into a math lesson I couldn't crawl out of. But it is important to understand that the equation basically says that there is a definite relationship between raw energy (we could call it power) and physical things, that physical things contain an immense amount of energy for their size, and that, theoretically, physical stuff could be converted into that raw energy.

That theory became demonstrated fact in the development and explosion of the first atomic bomb having the power to devastate an entire city by releasing the energy from just 137 pounds of uranium. It was a tragic scene against which the shocked world learned that matter could actually be converted into energy. Most have agreed that its use as an explosive is too much power for anyone to have, and the world lives in fear that it may happen again. The few pounds of material in nuclear reactors that power entire cities is still dangerous power when not confined.

We wonder how the power to level an entire city could be crammed into such a small amount of material and who could have crammed it there? Who has the arm strong enough to compress that power into every 100 pounds of material in the entire earth? (The mass of the earth is capable of producing a number of atomic bombs equal to one with twenty-two zeros—an inconceivable number and unimaginable power.) So how could power be stored in matter?

What if the equation went backward? What if it could be reversed so that energy could be converted into matter? What if we saw the film run backward and an entire city was created from a white-hot mushroom cloud before our eyes? Is it so

How could power be stored in matter?

fantastic to believe that God could reverse the process, creating matter out of His Own Great Energy?

What do we think happened when He said, "Let there be light"? Remember that light has everything to do with Einstein's equation. It seems to be the bridge between energy and material. God spoke the heavens and the earth into existence, not out of nothing, but . . .

> He has made the earth by His power;
> He has established the world by His wisdom,
> And stretched out the heaven by His understanding.
>
> Jeremiah 51:15 (NKJV)

He stuffed energy into matter in the first place, we only recently discovering the immense power knitting the universe together. He did not start with nothing; He started with something, and that something has everything to do with Who and What He is.

> The voice of the Lord [is] powerful;
> The voice of the Lord [is] full of majesty.
>
> Psalm 29:4 (NKJV)

Creation at Its Roots

The notion that true creation, that a real creative act, demands that something appear, poof!, out of nothing may be difficult to abandon. After all, men make things out of other things, but we are hesitant to call it "creation." We label the works of men "creative" or "unique," but we think to ourselves that certainly they are not real creation. We know we can't do what God did, and we want a distinction to be drawn. How are God's creative acts to be understood?

> In the beginning God *created* the heavens and the earth.
>
> Genesis 1:1 (NKJV); italics added

This word *created* is the Hebrew word *bara* and occurs fifty-four times in the Old Testament. Other instances help fix the meaning of this first one in Genesis.

> And the Lord God formed man [of] the dust of the ground, and breathed into his nostrils the breath of life; and man became a living being.
>
> Genesis 2:7 (NKJV)

The record is clear that Adam was formed from the soil, that is, God formed him from something else that already existed. How is this formation characterized?

> This is the book of the genealogy of Adam. In the day that God *created* man, He made him in the likeness of God.
>
> Genesis 5:1 (NKJV)

Adam's formation in 2:7 is characterized by the word *created* (bara) in 5:1. There are other examples,[95] but this is sufficient to show that the essence of creation is to start with something in the first place. Forming Adam from the soil was creation. We could easily be drawn to believe that God created Adam as an original from whom the rest of us are just copies off the reproductive assembly line, not really created in the true sense. The psalmist puts that idea to rest when he says . . .

> You send forth Your Spirit, they are *created*; And You renew the face of the earth.
>
> Psalm 104:30 (NKJV); italics added

You guessed it. There is that Hebrew word *bara* again just as it was "in the day God created man." Each human that is born is

---

[95]   See Isaiah 43:15; Isaiah 57:19; Psalm 102:18 as other examples

truly a new creation. We are no less a miracle of creation than was
Adam or Eve. God, of course, goes well

> *To create; make something out of something*

beyond human creative capability because
He took the soil He formed and breathed
into it the breath of life. That does not
change the root meaning of creation,
which is to "make a new form from
something that already exists." In that sense, mankind constantly
participates in real creation, and no surprise, since he was made in
the likeness and Image of God.[96]

When Men Create

The best of men's creations are done with passion and energy. For
each of us, passion is tied to our talents. It might be a poem, a
song, handcrafted furniture, or a garden. We could be creative at
decorating, cooking, football, or public speaking.

Most of us have a past work where our talent fused with our
passion to produce more than we expected. In it we invested our
deep emotion and expressed a piece of ourselves. It takes risk to
put such personal commitment into our labors. What if people
don't like it? What if I don't like it? What if my best isn't good
enough? To unveil it publicly is to bare part of our soul. Glimpses
into our core being, what makes us tick, become open to scrutiny.
We are vulnerable to reactions ranging from applause to apathy
to outright scorn.

We look at the ceiling of the Sistine Chapel with awe and
amazement. We don't think about the hours of labor, the endless
scaffold climbing, checking perspective, adjusting theme, testing
color. We can't much appreciate what must have been eye-
straining, back-wrenching, neck-bending work. Michelangelo
probably thought little of it himself. When he looked up, instead
of work to be done, he saw a great theme to unveil, a great story

---

[96]   Genesis 1:26, Colossians 1:15

to be told, a majestic God to unfold. His work displays a grand passion and vision that refused to stay inside.

How might it have cut Michelangelo if the reaction to his painting of the Sistine Chapel had been, "So?" Being ignored or openly criticized for a labor close to our hearts is difficult to bear. It is worse still to have the work of our hands greatly acclaimed yet credited to someone else. In fact, in showing his great earlier work, the *Pieta*, done at the age of twenty-three, Michelangelo was faced with exactly that situation. We read from the history, "When it was unveiled a proud Michelangelo stood by and watched as people admired the beautiful *Pieta*. What was pride turned into anger as he overheard a group of people attributing the work to other artists of his time. That anger caused Michelangelo to add one last thing to his sculpture. Going down the sash on the Virgin Mary, Michelangelo carved his name."[97] Like Michelangelo, how offended we are when someone else gets credit for our work.

Evolution maintains that there was no thoughtful, intelligent, purposeful being who created what we see. Our world, our universe is sheer happenstance. *Nothing* created the heavens and the earth. Can you imagine how it must offend God to be scorned as a bystander or credit evolution instead of Him? He Who invested His very nature, Who demonstrated His love in His creation is pushed aside as a nonentity. But like Michelangelo, He will not have it.

> I have made the earth,
> And created man on it.
> I—My hands—stretched out the heavens,
> And all their host I have commanded.
>
> Isaiah 45:12 (NKJV)

Mankind would erase His name from His work, would use science to obscure God's hand rather than discover it, would

---

[97] Anthony Parente, www.italiansrus.com

ignore the evidence that abounds at every turn. God's wrath is brewing against the darkened hearts of mankind.

> For God's indignation is being revealed from heaven on all the irreverence and injustice of men who are retaining the truth in injustice, because that which is known of God is apparent among them, for God manifests it to them. For His invisible attributes are descried from the creation of the world, being apprehended by His achievements, besides His imperceptible power and divinity, for them to be defenseless, because, knowing God, not as God do they glorify or thank Him, but vain were they made in their reasonings, and darkened is their unintelligent heart.
>
> Romans 1:18–21 (CLV)

God repeatedly reminds us that creation is His work and shows us how to recognize His signature.

> Lift your eyes and look to the heavens:
> Who created all these?
> He who brings out the starry host one by one,
> and calls them each by name.
> Because of his great power and mighty strength,
> not one of them is missing.
>
> Isaiah 40:26 (NIV)

Are we slow of heart to comprehend and believe ALL that God has said?[98] Evolutionists, in the end, believe in things springing out of nothing. We might ask, "Where did the super-dense particle come from to provide the big bang?" Since pure evolutionary thought cannot admit to God, consistency demands one answer, "Out of nothing." Ironically, evolutionists like to level this argument against Christians: "The extent of the [creationist's]

---

[98]   Luke 24:25]

scientific explanation for the beginning of life is POOF!"[99] My dear evolutionist friend, try this on for size.

> The Lord [is] slow to anger and great in power,
> And will not at all acquit [the] [wicked].
> The Lord has His way
> In the whirlwind and in the storm,
> And the clouds [are] the dust of His feet.
> He rebukes the sea and makes it dry,
> And dries up all the rivers.
> Bashan and Carmel wither,
> And the flower of Lebanon wilts.
> The mountains quake before Him,
> The hills melt,
> And the earth heaves at His presence,
> Yes, the world and all who dwell in it.
>
> Nahum 1:3–5 (NKJV)

Poof!, indeed! If we tussle with evolutionists about who believes more in things springing out of nothing, we only poorly point to God. Proclaiming that God made things out of nothing is a poor substitute for what He really did. We have been duped into the "out of nothing" idea. Maybe it just isn't the way we think it is.

All truly and literally has its source in God. The definition of creation is to form the new from the existing. The very stuff of the universe is "out of God." "Out of nothing" is the evolutionary idea, the atheistic idea.

> And the light shines in the darkness, and the darkness did not comprehend it.
>
> John 1:5 NASB

---

[99] Lenny Flank, "What is the 'Scientific Theory of Creation'?" [for article] OR *What is the "Scientific Theory of Creation"?* [for book title] 1996.

We don't expect those that deny God to understand, but Christians should understand the truth and the truth is that everything starts with something. All things came from Something, and without Something, nothing came into being that has come into being. All came out of Yahweh Who is and Who was. The profound lesson points back to a God always having filled the universe with His presence. There was never *nothing* for as far back as the heart can see. There was always God, Yahweh by name. That is a living God we can rely upon.[100]

If and when the skeptics come, we give them the right answer that all is "out of God," we might perhaps save some.[101] They must come to see that between the two ideas of origins, from nothing or from God, there is a world of difference and a worldly difference.

How satisfying it is that a God Who created us moves seamlessly between energy and matter. At the sight of Christ riding into Jerusalem, the crowds burst into praise saying, "Blessed is the King Who comes in the name of the Lord!"[102] But the Pharisees scolded them and told the Teacher to quiet His followers.

But He answered and said to them, "I tell you that if these should keep silent, the stones would immediately cry out."

Luke 19:40 (NKJV)

We have thought this a figure of speech. We may have said to ourselves, "What a great metaphor to personify the stones as if they would break into praise." Perhaps it isn't a metaphor after all. Might the rocks literally sing His praise? The realization that God changed His own power and light into the substance of the

---

[100] Timothy 4:10
[101] Romans 11:14
[102] Luke 19:38

earth shows us why the rocks would cry out and the trees would clap for joy at the very presence of the Savior.[103] It is now more apparent how Christ took the form of a rock, a pillar of fire, a gush of water, when we know this substance was out of God and through Christ. All creation is compatible with, inhabitable by, and points back to the God from whom it came.

The stones would cry out

"Worthy art Thou, O Lord, our Lord and God,
To get glory and honor and power;
For Thou dost create all,
And because of Thy will they were, and are created."

Revelation 4:11 (CLV)

No wonder creation itself shouts out the glory of God. How must God be offended when the objects of His very love are dismissed as a mistake or as emanating from nothing?

(A Davidic Psalm)
The heavens are recounting the glory of El,
And the atmosphere is telling the work of His hands.
Day after day is uttering a saying,
And night after night is disclosing knowledge.
There is no audible saying, and there are no words;
Their voice is unheard.
Yet into the entire earth their voice goes forth,
And into the ends of the habitance their declarations.
For the sun, He has placed a tent in them,

Psalm 19:1–4 (CLV)

Ex nihilo has a ring of sophistication, of learnedness, yet it must be regarded for what it is, a frail manmade notion to describe the working of God. If we use God's own words to describe Him, He

---

[103]   Isaiah 55:12

cannot help but get the true glory He deserves. If we must have a phrase for God's creative work and the origin of all things, it should be the phrase in the original Greek of Scripture, *ta panta ek tou Theou,*[104] "all is out of God."

Man truly does create when he forms one thing from another. It is God's way. What we cannot do, what confounds our very imaginations and leaves us without words, is turn energy into substance and substance into life.

> Therefore I have uttered what I did not understand, Things too wonderful for me, which I did not know.
>
> Job 42:3b (NKJV)

Reflections

1. What two Scripture tests can be used to discover whether a proposed concept is valid?
2. Is the idea of creation coming *out of nothing* supported in the Bible? Why or why not?
3. If creation did not come out of nothing, what did it come out of?

4. According to scientific theory, how might God have generated the matter from which the universe is made?
5. How does the belief that true creation comes out of nothing impact the argument between Christians and evolutionists?

---

[104]   II Corinthians 5:18

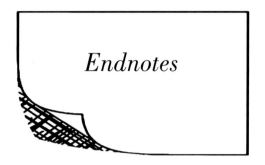

Endnotes

The Trinity: Help or Hindrance?

i.   But aren't there things we can't understand about God? Of course there are. As Christian comedian Brad Stine put it, "If we could understand Him He wouldn't be God!"

On the other hand, if the trinity is in the Bible and we can't understand it, then what else is written that we can't understand? What is Scripture for? You see, the problem is that *confusion* around the trinity is put forth almost as a kind of proof. Who can argue with what none of us can understand? We are left with blind acceptance.

But what is the Scripture for?

> All scripture is inspired by God, and is beneficial for teaching, for exposure, for correction, for discipline in righteousness, 17 that the man of God may be equipped, fitted out for every good act.
>
> 2 Timothy 3:16 (CLV); italics added

Scripture is for enlightenment, for enhancing under-standing. It is beneficial for teaching. This tells us that those things written are understand*able*. We don't understand every inch of Scripture, far from it. But what is there *can* be understood. There is much about God we don't and won't understand. But Scripture doesn't present those subjects. How well does it describe heaven? Hardly at all. Scripture isn't mystical and is not intended to be. Else how could we "Rightly divide the word of truth" (2 Timothy 2:15) and why should we? If we must accept that the trinity just can't be understood, then we can hide behind the same argument for any doctrine that frustrates us.

ii.   The "three are one" is not in the original Biblical text. The following is taken from Robert Nguyen Cramer, BibleTexts.com.
http://www.bibletexts.com/kjv-tr.htm#1jo0507
1 John 5:7, 8—an example of textual corruption. Even up to the fifth and final edition of Erasmus' Greek text in 1535, Erasmus occasionally fell prey to pressure from Roman Catholic church authorities to add to subsequent editions phrases and entire verses that he strongly (and rightly) suspected were not part of the original text. Metzger (*Ibid.*, pages 100–101) and others document how Erasmus was manipulated to include what later was translated into the KJV in 1 John 5:7–8, the following text: "in heaven, the Father, the Word, and the Holy Ghost; and these three are one. And there are three that bear witness in earth." Conservative biblical scholar F. F. Bruce (*History of the English Bible, Third Edition*, New York: Oxford University Press, 1978, pages 141–142) explains the sad history of how those words were errantly added to Erasmus' Greek text of 1 John 5:7–8:

The words ["in heaven, the Father, the Word, and the Holy Ghost; and these three are one. And there are three that bear witness in earth."] omitted in the R.V. [*Revised Version*, 1881] were no part of the original Greek text, nor yet of the Latin Vulgate in its earliest form. They first appear in the writings of a Spanish Christian leader named Priscillian, who was executed for heresy in A.D. 385. Later they made their way into copies of the Latin text of the Bible. When Erasmus prepared his printed edition of the Greek New Testament, he rightly left those words out, but was attacked for this by people who felt that the passage was a valuable proof-text for the doctrine of the Trinity. He replied (rather incautiously) that if he could be shown any Greek manuscript which contained the words, he would include them in his next edition. Unfortunately, a Greek manuscript not more than some twenty years old was produced in which the words appeared: they had been translated into Greek from Latin. Of course, the fact that the only Greek manuscript exhibiting the words belonged to the sixteenth century was in itself an argument against their authenticity, but Erasmus had given his promise, and so in his 1522 edition he included the passage. (To-day one or two other very late Greek manuscripts are known to contain this passages; all others omit it.)

[For more details on Erasmus' addition of the 1 John 5:7, 8 text, see Metzger's *The Text of the New Testament, Second Edition*, pages 101–102 and also http://www.bibletexts.com/versecom/1jo05v07.htm.]

iii. Translational differences of *firstborn of all creation*
Some of the newer translations including the New International Version and the New King James render this passage, "Firstborn *over* all creation." Would this change

be more comfortable for the trinity viewpoint? Perhaps. It gives the sense that Christ is *first* in *authority* over creation, which might remove Him from being amongst the class of creatures. If we examine the use of *firstborn*, we will find that it has the sense of first with others to follow. Three verses later (Colossians 1:18), He is said to be t*he firstborn from among the dead.* We understand from this that others will also be raised to immortality from the dead, but He was first. He was also first of all creatures, but other creatures were to follow. But there are no others to *follow* in His authority. He cannot be *firstborn over all creation* with others to follow. Therefore translating using the word *over* all creation instead of using *of* all creation misleads the intent of the passage and the meaning of firstborn. However, it is a convenient change for those who want to support the idea that Christ was not a created being as this conflicts with the trinity.

The foregoing argument is rather unneeded since the word over is not in the Greek text. The word creation or creature is in the genitive case, which is why almost all older translations render it firstborn of all creation or firstborn of every creature.